SOCIAL WORK PRACTICE, 1970

SOCIAL WORK PRACTICE, 1970

SELECTED PAPERS, 97TH ANNUAL FORUM

NATIONAL CONFERENCE ON SOCIAL WELFARE

CHICAGO, ILLINOIS, MAY 31–JUNE 5, 1970

 Published 1970 for the

NATIONAL CONFERENCE ON SOCIAL WELFARE *by*

COLUMBIA UNIVERSITY PRESS, *New York and London*

Copyright © 1970
National Conference on Social Welfare, Columbus, Ohio
Published by Columbia University Press

ISBN: 0-231-03474-1
Library of Congress Catalog Card Number: 5-35377

PRINTED IN THE UNITED STATES OF AMERICA

The Contributors

ELAINE BRODY, Director, Department of Social Work, Philadelphia Geriatric Center, Philadelphia; Principal Investigator, "Individualized Treatment of Mentally Impaired Aged," NIMH Grant #15047

HARRIS CHAIKLIN, Professor, School of Social Work, University of Maryland, Baltimore

LEON W. CHESTANG, Director of Casework Studies, Child and Family Services, Chicago

ARTHUR C. EMLEN, Professor of Social Work, State University School of Social Work, Portland, Oreg.; Project Director, Field Study of the Neighborhood Family Day Care System

CHARLES GARVIN, Associate Professor, School of Social Work, University of Michigan, Ann Arbor

PAUL GLASSER, Professor of Social Work, School of Social Work, University of Michigan, Ann Arbor

ARCHIE HANLAN, Associate Professor, School of Social Work, University of Pennsylvania, Philadelphia

BETTY A. KIRBY, casework student, Graduate School of Social Work, University of Denver, Denver

PAUL A. KURZMAN, Director, Neighborhood Youth Corps, Human Resources Administration, New York

CHARLES LONG, Vocational Rehabilitation Specialist, Community Addiction Treatment Center, Washington, D.C.

GLENN W. OLSON, Executive Director, Alta House, Cleveland

AUDREY PITTMAN, Assistant Professor, School of Social Administration, Temple University, Philadelphia

NORMA RADIN, Assistant Professor, School of Social Work, University of Michigan, Ann Arbor

LAWRENCE SHULMAN, Assistant Professor, McGill University School of Social Work, Montreal, Canada

HERBERT A. SILVERMAN, Chief Research Social Worker, "Individualized Treatment of Mentally Impaired Aged," NIMH grant MH 15047

JEFFREY R. SOLOMON, President, Social Consult, Inc., New York
CAROL H. WEISS, Research Associate, Bureau of Applied Social Research, Columbia University, New York
HAROLD H. WEISSMAN, Assistant Professor, Hunter College School of Social Work, New York; formerly Assistant Executive Director, Mobilization for Youth, New York

The National Conference on Social Welfare

THE NATIONAL CONFERENCE ON SOCIAL WELFARE is a voluntary organization of individual and organizational members whose major function is to provide a national forum for the critical examination of basic problems and issues in the social welfare field.

These annual forums furnish a two-way channel of communication between paid and volunteer workers, between social welfare and allied fields, and between the service organizations and the social work profession.

Since 1874, through its annual forums and its comprehensive publications program, the National Conference has reflected the history and dynamic development of social welfare in this country. Its national office serves as headquarters for state conferences in social welfare; as the secretariat for the U.S. Committee of the International Council on Social Welfare; and as a clearinghouse for educational materials for use on local, state, national, and international levels.

Among the newer services developed by the Conference in recent years is its insurance program and information services, including a library of unpublished Annual Forum manuscripts; its document retrieval program, of which the data-processed production of the *KWIC Index* of its publications since 1874 is a part; and its selected bibliography service.

Foreword

A GLANCE AT THE Contents and Abstracts of this volume indicates the wide range of practice dealt with in the papers chosen from the large number presented. In our judgment, the subject matter demonstrates that the field is actively attempting to test in practice many of the broad issues under dispute in the policy and program areas. In every component of practice there seems to be a practical relevancy to the tempestuous times in which we live. As we apply our skills, it is imperative that we continue to report our specific experience because, from these successes or failures, broad policy can be tested and evaluated. It is from these applications that disputed issues will finally be decided. With these observations, the Editorial Committee expresses, on behalf of the National Conference on Social Welfare, deep appreciation to all who prepared papers for the 1970 Forum and to the staff for their efficient assistance.

JAY L. RONEY
CHAIRMAN, SUBCOMMITTEE
OF THE EDITORIAL COMMITTEE

Contents

THE CONTRIBUTORS	v
THE NATIONAL CONFERENCE ON SOCIAL WELFARE	vii
FOREWORD *Jay L. Roney*	ix
ABSTRACTS	xiii
A CONSERVATIVE STRATEGY FOR SOCIAL PLANNING IN THE SEVENTIES *Harold H. Weissman*	3
CLIENT, STAFF, AND THE SOCIAL AGENCY *Lawrence Shulman*	21
FROM SOCIAL WORK TO SOCIAL ADMINISTRATION *Archie Hanlan*	41
ALLEVIATING TENSIONS IN AN ETHNIC NEIGHBORHOOD *Glenn W. Olson*	54
BEYOND ADVOCACY: A NEW MODEL FOR COMMUNITY ORGANIZATION *Paul A. Kurzman* and *Jeffrey R. Solomon*	65
ETHICAL AND POLITICAL ISSUES IN SOCIAL RESEARCH *Carol H. Weiss*	74
INDIVIDUALIZED TREATMENT OF THE MENTALLY IMPAIRED AGED *Elaine Brody* and *Herbert A. Silverman*	89
A SOCIAL SERVICE TEAM FOR PUBLIC WELFARE *Harris Chaiklin*	103
THE ISSUE OF RACE IN CASEWORK PRACTICE *Leon W. Chestang*	114

REALISTIC PLANNING FOR THE DAY CARE CONSUMER
   I. *Arthur C. Emlen*   127
   II. *Audrey Pittman*   142

THE BASES OF SOCIAL TREATMENT   *Charles Garvin* and *Paul Glasser*   149

GROUP FIELD WORK AND TUTORIAL EXPERIENCE *Betty A. Kirby*   178

PREVENTIVE INTERVENTION WITH LOW-INCOME FAMILIES THROUGH THE SCHOOL   *Norma Radin*   183

ADDICTION   *Charles Long*   198

INDEX   203

Abstracts

ELAINE BRODY and HERBERT A. SILVERMAN
"Individualized Treatment of the Mentally Impaired Aged"
Mental impairment in the elderly, defined as organic brain disorders affecting intellectual functioning, tends to endanger, physically or emotionally, the individual or those around him. Experiments conducted at the Philadelphia Geriatric Center under a NIMH grant have attempted through collaborative efforts of research, medicine, and social work to develop a foundation of data for evaluation of both treatment and services. Results have established substantial information on the effects of positive change in functioning following treatment of excessive disabilities, on predictors of improvement, and on guides to most effective treatments.

HARRIS CHAIKLIN
"A Social Service Team for Public Welfare"
Evidence of a Baltimore cooperative casework-community organization experiment in family living indicates that physically improved living conditions may tend to increase psychosocial problems; that increased income alone will not stabilize the process of family deterioration. Policy-makers in public welfare must find means to improve both the material and the socioemotional lives of recipients; must use the present system as a base for making even the most radical changes; and must accept that the poor will not wait for endless debate in search of miraculous solutions.

LEON W. CHESTANG
"The Issue of Race in Casework Practice"
Blacks, no longer accepting the myth of white supremacy, are questing for self-determination and community control, for the right to define themselves *by* themselves. Social work must understand and accept that the major problem is racism—not poverty or cultural deprivation. What may appear to be dysfunction in black families may well be an

expression of great strength in a hostile society where power is rooted in the ability to control and the idealized family stereotype is represented by the permanently employed father and the homemaker mother striving for affluence and social status.

ARTHUR C. EMLEN
"Realistic Planning for the Day Care Consumer: I"
Recent research contradicts the assumption, often based on carelessly defined needs, that more day care facilities will solve day care needs; questions agency emphasis on organized day care programs and disparagement of neighborhood homes or sitters chosen by working mothers. Professional concern for child development too often contrasts the worst of family planned care with the best in agency-supervised centers and ignores utilization behavior and rights of mothers to reject agency facilities in favor of neighborhood care as an extension of family with a potential for enriching the lives of children.

CHARLES GARVIN and PAUL GLASSER
"The Bases of Social Treatment"
"Social treatment," merging the best elements of casework and group work methods, concentrates on diagnostic and treatment methods chosen to meet the needs of clients and is especially adaptable to treatment of nonvoluntary deviants. Procedural steps are: diagnosis; goal determination; intervention plan; the helping contract; means of influence which may be direct worker efforts to modify behavior; indirect change through group participation or worker extra-group influence in environmental change; and evaluation.

ARCHIE HANLAN
"From Social Work to Social Administration"
Social welfare administrators, identified as symbols of an unresponsive establishment, often adopt characteristics of administrative activists, using strategies of conflict to bring system change in social welfare. Three models are discussed in relation to overlapping functions and adaptability for accomplishing political, social, and economic change: the social work administrator, closely related to professional patterns and knowledge; the social welfare model, directed toward formation of social policy and improvement of social functioning; and the Western European model of social administration, focusing on national development and distribution of national resources.

BETTY A. KIRBY
"Group Field Work and Tutorial Experience"
A student reports on a three-year University of Denver experiment in

Abstracts

utilization of the field teaching center concept for first year students followed by second year tutorial experience. Major advantages include group support in relieving student anxiety and development of professional confidence and identification; accelerated theoretical learning; and development of initiative and independence. Disadvantages include retarded development of professional skills, which tend to fall below agency expectations, and some overdependency on supervisors.

PAUL A. KURZMAN and JEFFREY R. SOLOMON
"Beyond Advocacy: a New Model for Community Organization"
Professional workers in developing means of community organization must go beyond their traditional role as enabler or the more aggressive role as advocate to a new function in strengthening client self-determination and developing self-reliance within the community. A "research consultant" model proposes worker involvement in three phases: as "organizer-advocate," stimulating change through system confrontation; as "organizer-educator," with the client gradually assuming the role of self-advocacy; and as "organizer-technical assistant" with the worker remaining invisible as an adviser.

CHARLES LONG
"Addiction"
A former addict sees drug addiction as a sickness, the only sickness punishable by law, with the addict as a helpless victim. He denies that pushers are responsible for youth addiction and blames personality and emotional or environmental conflict instead. Addiction, once established, controls its victim through his mental attitudes and his fear of "the sickness" described vividly as the "most horrible of all sicknesses." His greatest need is acceptance and understanding from those better able to face realities and for improved public education and information through churches, schools, and other organizations.

GLENN W. OLSON
"Alleviating Tensions in an Ethnic Neighborhood"
Successful application of "sensible politics" in testing neighborhood control of community development as a means of overcoming the violence of ethnic subcultures in Cleveland's "Little Italy" was initially threatened by failure to identify and use "true" leaders of the community. Hostile opposition, overcome by involvement of these newly emerged leaders in power positions, has brought new support for the project, physical improvement in the neighborhood, and new hope for healthy collaboration in resolving racial conflict and the violence of ethnic reactions.

AUDREY PITTMAN
"Realistic Planning for the Day Care Consumer: II"
Basic conclusion of "Operation Alphabet," a Philadelphia project under Title V of the Economic Opportunity Act, was that agency models for child care could not be imposed on unwilling AFDC working mothers. Initial goal "to expand approved day care centers" was altered to "the assessment and improvement of existing 'mother-selected' plans," recognizing the mother as the initiator in providing her own baby-sitter or neighborhood home care, with the worker becoming a welcome consultant in solving problems or evaluating such arrangements.

NORMA RADIN
"Preventive Intervention with Low-Income Families through the School"
School social workers are suggested as best qualified to develop and coordinate problem-preventive programs for potential school failures. Effective functioning will depend on worker recognition of the eagerness among low-income parents for school success for their children; of their lack of skills and knowledge needed to provide home help in developing school competence. Parent-education programs should stress skills related to control of child behavior and decision-making, and should emphasize the strength of participants and the mutual exchange of ideas rather than the traditional therapeutic relationship between worker and parent.

LAWRENCE SHULMAN
"Client, Staff, and the Social Agency"
Agency productivity is directly related to communication between levels of authority with the executive as principal catalyst influencing effectiveness through staff development. The supervisor becomes the "common ground" between administration and staff, assuming a double identity—as an agency member interacting with other staff and as a professional in client relations. Social agency systems must try different strategies and record results of staff response, positive or negative, that has diminishing effectiveness in attaining agency objectives.

CAROL H. WEISS
"Ethical and Political Issues in Social Research"
Resistance to social research poses ethical questions involving the health, privacy, and anonymity of the subject who tends to question motives of the sponsoring power and the uses of research results. The

research community, to avoid intolerable outside censorship, must insure protection of human dignity, must consider the physical and psychological effects of proposed studies on subjects and his social group, and through frank discussion of the meaning and uses of data get the "informed consent" of each human subject.

HAROLD H. WEISSMAN
"A Conservative Strategy for Social Planning in the Seventies"
Social planners must first win the commitment of an overwhelming majority of American citizens—must create public awareness of the benefits to society in return for expenditure of time and money. Revolutionary tactics, conflict, and confrontation have brought public resistance but have offered no solutions. The social work profession, too long allied with liberals and radicals, must recognize "consumer sovereignty" in the options of a free society, must admit the efficiencies of private enterprise, and recognize that not all power and authority is corrupt. Flexibility must be built into social planning to compensate for our limited knowledge and to deal with emergencies.

SOCIAL WORK PRACTICE, 1970

A Conservative Strategy for Social Planning in the Seventies

HAROLD H. WEISSMAN

THERE IS A GROWING FEELING among some social workers, as well as among the population as a whole, that once one becomes aware of the problems which exist in our society only two courses are open: increasing militancy or apathy. Several factors suggest the validity of such a position. One contributing factor is that spokesmen for other viewpoints have often been either overly defensive or crudely inarticulate. This is especially so as regards a conservative position in social work, since such a viewpoint has always been looked upon by the field as somewhat illegitimate, if not outright subversive. Yet, it may be that the seventies will favor a conservative philosophy, though one that differs considerably from Social Darwinism, strict constructionism, or an apology for racial repression.

The decade of the sixties was one of rapid change in social welfare, best characterized as a shift from concern with individual change to concern with social change. New methods of service delivery, such as neighborhood service centers, a new conception of the role of the social worker as advocate, and renewed emphasis on social action in community organization came to the fore. These changes resulted in part from plans and projections made by social workers at the beginning of the decade in such projects as Mobilization for Youth and the Ford Foundation's grey areas programs, and in part from adaptations to unanticipated changes in social conditions.[1]

---

[1] See *A Proposal for the Prevention and Control of Delinquency by Expanding Opportunities* (New York: Mobilization for Youth, 1969); Peter Marris and Martin Rein, *Dilemmas of Social Reform* (New York: Atherton Press, 1967).

The experience of the decade was salutary for social work. The defense of the welfare system ceased to be part of our "oath of allegiance." The fact that a great deal of what social workers do does not require a master's degree suddenly became obvious. The poor were not necessarily hard to reach.

Yet, there is abiding reason to be less sanguine about the effects of the changes on our clients. We are not yet adequately educating the slum child; housing in the center city is deteriorating at an astronomical pace; community control over local institutions is of limited value if these institutions have insufficient resources to achieve their goals. As the seventies begin, there is a distinct skepticism, even a distrust, of liberals and liberal policies. William Pfaff states it thus:

The most important political and social anxieties felt today within the industrial societies fall outside the traditional categories of the left. They no longer are economic issues, and the tradition of the left has been to define politics in economic and class categories. They are issues like identity and social community, recalling past conservative critiques of industrial and urban society. These new anxieties express an ambivalence about technology—the source of egalitarian affluence—and a reaction (often blind, increasingly influential) against the centralization of authority in modern society, the anonymity of power, and—perhaps most of all—power's seeming escape from reasonable control.[2]

It is my major argument that the policies and procedures of the sixties, from the confrontation with governmental agencies to the delineation of power as the motive force of social change, can be liabilities in terms of securing the resources required for change, especially so in the quiescent periods which usually follow eras of reform as well as wars, when the major problem is one of sustaining a social sanction for change. The strategies and tactics of the sixties were natural outgrowths of social welfare's long alliance with liberal and radical political groups. In order to construct a more appropriate set of tactics for the post-Vietnam period, the bases of this past alliance as well as its shortcomings must be understood.

[2] William Pfaff, "The Decline of Liberal Politics," *Commentary*, XLVIII, No. 4 (1969), 46.

A Conservative Strategy for Social Planning

VALUE JUDGMENTS AND THE SANCTION FOR CHANGE

Kahn points out that "real value issues, about which there may be legitimate differences, are at the heart of planning."[3] They clearly determine what is sanctioned.

> It has been argued with considerable force and merit that the characteristic activity in a planning process is choosing. . . . Although one should not downgrade the research, the fact-finding, the programming, the practice innovation, or the evaluation and feedback, a convincing and impressive case can certainly be made for such an emphasis. . . .
>
> Opinions, beliefs, values, choices are very much in the forefront in planning.[4]

A profession's value judgments are difficult to question. Nevertheless, if we are to affect the way in which society allocates its resources in the seventies, it is of crucial importance to understand these judgments and evaluate them in terms of how they affect the public's willingness to sanction social change.

Human motivation. At the core of many policy disagreements is the matter of belief in the perfectibility of human beings and of society. Broadly, liberals view human beings as educable, desirous of doing good, and amenable to change through love and opportunity. Conservatives tend to see people as needing control and authority, as much motivated by fear as by love, and perhaps more inclined toward social evil than toward good. Liberals are more concerned about the needs of individuals; conservatives, about the needs of society.

Social planners have, in the main, accepted the liberal view. The issue is clearly one of preference rather than of an objective evaluation. Social work as a profession has never really attempted systematically to organize its experience with human behavior. Social workers have been mainly preoccupied with translating the actions, attitudes, and emotions of their clients into therapeutic languages. What social workers have not done is to develop out of their experience a psychology of everyday life, a psychology of

---

[3] Alfred J. Kahn, *Theory and Practice of Social Planning* (New York: Russell Sage Foundation, 1969), p. 113.

[4] *Ibid.*, p. 97. Henceforth, the designation "planners" will be used to refer to social workers engaged in devising social welfare policies and programs.

how people operate in the workaday world that would guide policy choices. Planners have thus been left to devise social programs, all of which are grounded in a social psychology, on the basis of their professional intuition about how people act, guidelines provided by various therapeutically oriented psychological theories, or what they have gained from liberal historians and political philosophers.

Such psychological theories seemingly have not alerted planners to the fact that, justifiably or unjustifiably, husbands will desert their wives so that they may get welfare. They do not account for the fact that many programs are weakened because of the nature of a free society and the options it offers.

Integration in schools, for example, cannot succeed perfectly because people are able to move to the suburbs or to send their children to private schools; thus efforts to promote integration which do not take into account these options may actually perpetuate segregation. In a free society people have options, and they exercise these in ways which often run counter to the requisites of social programs.

There are other gaps in the liberal viewpoint. One important question around which a great deal of debate about social welfare revolves is how much help is necessary, as well as what kinds of demands should be placed on those receiving help. By and large, social workers have felt that society has no right to make great demands on the poor because it is society that makes people poor in the first place. Yet, planners, in their valid concern with protecting the poor from overly harsh demands have been inclined to simplify the relationship between individuals and society. They emphasize the theory that society is the nurturant of the individual and they show considerably less concern for the fact that the individual is actually as much a nurturant of society as society's institutions are.

Institutional change, therefore, has of late been a major concern of liberal planners. Yet, they err in assuming that the speed and direction of individual change is commensurate with that of institutional change. Transform a custodially oriented prison into a rehabilitative one, and the prisoners will still tend to "con" the system. The inability to consider the necessity of programmatically accounting for such a lag, which stems from a liberal conception of human interaction, has resulted in many programs that, by and large, are ineffective. This is especially dangerous in America where the political right has not been distinguished for providing alternatives, but merely for obstructing the left. There is a crisis in public confidence in government measures:

Underlying the surface debates—gurantned income versus black capitalism, bureaucratic reform versus community control, politicization of the poor communities versus programs of family support and social welfare—is deep uncertainty over what any of these programs can really accomplish. Whether it is justified or not—and in considerable measure it may be unjustified—there is among the public a persistent sense of the futility of such measures.[5]

Task preferences. Planners tend to denigrate the value of amelioration of symptoms in their desire to deal with root causes. While reasonable, this strategy is also based on the fear that, for example, if, through police surveillance, all the addicts in one neighborhood were chased to another, nothing else would be done by the public to solve the problem. Perhaps this would be the case.

Yet, short-range, ameliorative solutions are quite rational. There is as yet no known way to deal adequately with the drug problem. Thus, the preferences of planners to deal with basic causes and to offer long-run solutions without giving short-run assistance can result in frustration and, ultimately, public lack of support or sanction for longer-range programs.

A second basic task preference, also an understandable one, is simply to plan programs.

Planning is not always appropriate. . . . Societies must respond rapidly to emergencies, must give scope to impulse and intuition. . . . In fact, extravagance must also be allowed its place in the total configuration. Furthermore, the protection of core values may at times preclude any type of social bookkeeping.

[5] Pfaff, *op. cit.*. Some of the public's misgivings may be based on their intuition about the psychology that underlies many of the programs. For example, client contributions are often considered by social workers as akin to punishment or as a device to screen out the needy rather than as something that society requires and people wish to make. Opposing the negative use of contributions as screening devices is valid; refusing to consider the positive uses is self-defeating.

Nor is planning always possible even when appropriate. Major social problems may cry out for solution, and fragmented programs may appear in desperate need of coordination; but little can be expected unless a sanction for planning exists or can be created. . . .

Feasibility is also limited at times by the realities of resources, knowledge, technique, and ability to project.[6]

Behind this inclination to plan is the premise that the expected utility of a program is sufficient to persuade the public to sanction whatever resources it may require. Lack of knowledge of how to create a sanction to plan is a severe limitation. Without it, planners are apt to accommodate to the limited resources available, which often leads to inappropriate programs and policies.

Policy preferences. Likewise, an inability to consider seriously how the desire for private gain can be utilized for social ends has caused errors in timing, misplaced priorities, and lost opportunities in planning social programs.[7] Planners too easily undervalue the role of private enterprise, voluntary activity, and informality, since these are seldom amenable to planning. They clearly prefer governmental bureaucratic control with safeguards to assure fair and efficient administration. The public generally prefers to utilize private enterprise until it proves ineffective.

Only recently have planners begun to consider the utility of enabling clients to purchase services.[8] Many are also discovering that it is easier to effect compromises when money values can be placed on the issues involved in a dispute than when issues remain solely at the level of ideals. No one compromises ideals easily; witness the refusal of some planners to consider the potential efficiency of private enterprise until the recent financial pinch on social services.

A related ideal is the desire of social planners to create a shared

---

[6] Kahn, *op. cit.*, pp. 328–29. For a stimulating discussion of the uses of mythology and prophecy as sanctions for planning, see John P. Sisk, "The Future of Prediction," *Commentary*, XLIX, No. 3 (1970), 65–68.

[7] "Greed is not a pretty motive, but it works, and the promoters of progress cannot afford to disdain it unless they are prepared, both philosophically and financially, to rely exclusively on governmental enterprise and capital." David F. Ross, as quoted by Eli Goldston, "New Prospects for American Business," *Daedalus*, XCVIII (1969), 96.

[8] Charles E. Lindblom, "The Rediscovery of the Market," *Public Interest*, No. 4 (1966), pp. 89–101.

basis of authority and leadership. Many planners are wedded to a concept of verbal democracy. The smoke-filled room gives way to the word-filled room. The idea that all that is needed to create a sanction for change is an opportunity for a dialogue between various groups and interests is a tremendous oversimplification. A dialogue may clarify issues; it can seldom suggest solutions acceptable to all parties. Without leadership and authority, dialogues often escalate conflicts to the point where democratic politics cannot resolve them.

Inherent in the above is a confusion concerning authoritarianism and the need for authority. The view that all power and all authority are inherently corrupt is related to a conception of human nature which relates man's foibles solely to the structure of the society. Heilbroner puts it as follows:

> The point . . . is not to counter the socialist vision with mutterings that man is vile. It is rather to insist that the deepest weakness of its vision has been its failure to formulate a conception of human behavior in all its historical, sociological, sexual, and ideational complexity, a conception that would present "man" as being at once biologic as well as social, tragic as well as heroic, limited as well as plastic.
>
> . . . .
>
> In a word, socialist thought, in its avoidance of the study of human behavior, has not directly faced the problem of how the individual is to be integrated into the community, or the degree to which individual behavior must be governed by social norms, or the appropriate boundaries between social and private spheres of existence. A fervent commitment to "participatory democracy" is today much voiced among Western socialist writers, but little or no consideration has been given to the means by which this participation can avoid what one commentator has called "the merciless masochism of community-minded and self-regulating men and women." (Oscar Wilde once remarked that socialism would take too many evenings, and the quip deserves to be taken seriously.) [9]

The one clear case in which an authoritarian social system was changed to a democratic one occurred through the use first of procedures based on authority.[10]

---

[9] Robert L. Heilbroner, "Socialism and the Future," *Commentary*, XLVIII, No. 6 (1969), 43, 44. This article also contains rejoinders to the above criticisms.

[10] Allen R. Holmberg, "Participant Intervention in the Field," *Human Organiza-*

Program preferences. In developing programs, liberal planners show a decided preference for "compensatory justice." Yet, no matter how much agreement there is that black people have been persecuted in the past, there is little likelihood that the majority of whites will feel responsible for these persecutions and will be willing to give up any of their gains, many of which were hard earned.[11]

To press the drive for compensatory justice, many social planners in the sixties sought to create social organizations, if not a social movement of the poor, with the ability to muster a preponderance of political power in the inevitable bargaining which takes places in a democracy. Thus, they opposed the Moynihan Report, which had job training as its programmatic end, and opted for community action. Likewise, the psychological and political value to blacks of citizen participation and community control of local institutions is now considered by many planners as more important than an expanding economy and regional and nationwide economic and social programs.

Many social planners seem to believe that political organization must precede economic advancement for the poor.[12] In all probability, the two can only occur simultaneously. Experience shows

---

tion, XIV (1955), 23–26. Thoughtful revolutionaries, contrary to their rhetoric, know that society is ruled much more by legitimated authority than by power. Their tactic is constantly to undermine the legitimacy of authority so that only power remains. Of the two, the former is the more important adversary. The purposeful destruction of authority in the revolutionary sense is not the same as challenging authority in the reformist sense to meet its commitments.

[11] At a recent conference of urban white ethnic groups, Moynihan noted: "This is the group that, by and large, has been left out of the recent spate of government programs: if not forgotten, it is at least ignored . . . this—majority—group of Americans cannot but wonder what it is getting out of all the activity and, in particular, has to be asking whether the government is playing favorites, or greasing squeaky wheels or whatever. This is especially so because this group is anything but affluent. These are families that know where every half dollar goes." Absolute justice cannot always be paramount in formulating strategies of social change. Daniel P. Moynihan, quoted in *The Reacting Americans* (New York: American Jewish Committee, 1968), p. 7.

[12] A variety of strategies and activities is required to sustain a social movement which inevitably will conflict with the need to achieve immediate substantive results. For a full discussion of this point, see Harold H. Weissman, "Epilogue," in Weissman, ed., *Justice and the Law in the Mobilization for Experience* (New York: Association Press, 1969), pp. 199–201.

A Conservative Strategy for Social Planning

that a considerable degree of economic stability is generally required if there is to be sustained political involvement.

An overcommitment in the seventies to any one political process, such as politicizing the poor, coupled with simplistic views about authority, governmental efficiency, the nature of a free society, and the relationship between institutions and individuals, will result in unsuccessful programs. These failures will severely limit the possibility of sustaining a sanction for social change.

Another limiting factor is the level of knowledge available about social planning itself. During the sixties the emphasis on rational centralized planning was attacked for its mechanistic, rigid, and authoritarian basis. Planning was seen as, at best, a precarious task, as indicated by the term used by many influential social planners, "disjointed incrementalism." Planning was to proceed by bits and pieces; there were too many variables to be controlled, too many unanticipated consequences, too much interplay between the various steps involved in carrying through plans. Planning was really the science of muddling through.[13] The best that could be achieved was small changes that did not risk too much harm to the body politic.

Kahn has recently charted a middle ground between the maximum planners and the marginalists, acknowledging openly that planning is certainly not the only source of social change and seldom qualifies as the predominant element.[14] He envisions the planning process as one of interrelated stages, feeding back one to the other, moving from the pivotal stage of definition of the planning task, to policy formulation, to programming, to evaluation and feedback, to redefinition, and so on.[15]

In delineating the planning process, Kahn acknowledges, but does not explicate, two key interrelated problems in planning: the mobilization of resources and the procurement of the sanc-

[13] For discussion of this point of view see, for example, Charles E. Lindblom, "The Science of Muddling Through," in Mayer N. Zald, ed., *Social Welfare Institutions* (New York: John Wiley & Sons, Inc., 1965), pp. 214–29.

[14] Kahn, *op. cit.*, p. 57.

[15] Amitai Etzioni, *The Active Society: a Theory of Social and Political Processes* (New York: Free Press, 1968), pp. 282–306, further explicates and provides a name for this model, "mixed scanning."

tion to plan—problems which promise to be crucial to progress in the seventies.

CHANGE IN A CYBERNETIC SOCIETY

In the sixties social workers focused their attention on mobilizing the resources of the central governing and guidance mechanism in society, the government, federal, city, and state. The institutional faces of government were confronted with their inadequacy. Lack of power on the part of the poor and minority groups was diagnosed as the cause of poverty. Confrontation and conflict were the tactics used to gain power.[16]

A fair reading of the results achieved, while open to argument over substantive achievements such as reducing poverty, cannot overlook the climate of concern created in the body politic for the social problems that enmesh it. Certainly, this tactic provided sanction for more planning and action than would have been dreamed possible at the beginning of the decade. The issue now is whether a tactic which was useful in creating a climate of concern will be as useful in mobilizing resources to attain desired social ends.

It is my thesis that dissensus politics can be counterproductive for such a mobilization, especially since resources other than money may have to be secured before money can be secured. For this latter task other governing mechanisms besides government itself will have to play an important role.

The seventies already present a disturbing picture: the population is growing; the atmosphere is being polluted; the cities are decaying; social problems are growing on a scale beyond comprehension. At the same time, the cost of services rises geometrically, as does the demand for different and varied services. What is on the decrease is the belief that government can solve the problems.

In the face of all this there is flashed that familiar list of programs: model cities, negative income tax, rent supplements, manpower development agencies, community mental health centers.

[16] See, for example, Richard A. Cloward and Frances Fox Piven, "Dissensus Politics: a Strategy for Winning Economic Rights," the *New Republic*, April 20, 1968, pp. 20-24.

A Conservative Strategy for Social Planning

The picture is completed by liberal politicians who bemoan the fiscal crisis of the cities.[17]

Yet it is abundantly clear that many problems, such as racism and its related evils, cannot be dealt with in the context of a free society unless there is a commitment on the part of the overwhelming majority of its citizens to do something about it. The same can probably be said about delinquency, about school dropouts, unemployment, and the like. It is not that such a commitment will immediately produce the needed funds, but that such commitments will release the public's concern and creativity from which social solutions as well as funds can emerge. This is not a mystical process.

MOBILIZATION OF RESOURCES

Implied in much of the criticism of liberal social preferences is another set of convictions: authority is necessary for social goals to be attained; the human concern for security and status is operative on all levels of society; the cost at times of solving certain social problems precludes the attempt to do so; amelioration is often the best that can be achieved; politicization of all aspects of community affairs ultimately stifles free speech, encourages simplification of issues, and undermines democracy. The value of these beliefs when translated into policies can only be judged in terms of their effectiveness in securing the resources during the seventies to make the poor, middle class—a somewhat unromantic goal to which they overwhelmingly subscribe.

Commitment. It is a fine line, and not merely semantics, as to whether one does away with delinquency or poverty in order to have a great society, or whether one must first have a great society to be able to do away with delinquency and poverty. Cer-

---

[17] One of the reasons that funds are not available is that social planners have adapted to their inability to secure ample funds (or the sanction to plan) by devising cheap programs, such as the war on poverty, that almost never have a real chance of succeeding. Thus, as time passes, no one really believes that the provision of more funds will solve the problems related to many social issues. Because political leadership cannot or will not distinguish for the public those areas where funds alone will assist in alleviating difficulties, and those areas where other resources are required, there is a tendency to treat it all, at best, as an exercise in futility.

tainly, the majority of a society, and not just a small percentage or one part of the political spectrum, must have a vision of its highest ideals if social problems are to be solved. This vision cannot be developed if professionals become permanent buffers between people and problems, witness the "invisible poor." The notion must be dispelled that social technicians of whatever professional stripe, social workers or policemen, singly or in cooperation, can themselves solve the social problems of our society; concomitantly, so also must be the idea that all they need to do the job is sufficient money. The liberal stand is, of course, that such frankness will only result in getting less money; therefore, an illusion of success has to be kept up. Very likely, this is not so.

It may be asked how, if social planners do not provide solutions to social problems, social change will come about. The best answer seems to be that they must continue to play this role while at the same time taking cognizance of the fact that too much emphasis on problems and on their own expertise ultimately can become counterproductive. A society must be aware of its social successes as well as of its problems if it is not to lose faith in itself and its ability to solve its problems. Social planners must sustain such a faith in individuals. This is the focal point of a conservative strategy for change.

Strategy. While there is a clear need for advocates for the oppressed, there is also a need for planners whose focus is on specific groups as well as on the whole society. While we are all demeaned by the condition of the poor, they may be even more demeaned by the condition of those who are not poor. In a democratic reformist society, substantial gains for the poor hinge considerably on the conditions, material and psychological, of more privileged groups, black and white.[18] This is a message which white social workers cannot easily bring to the black poor, and black social workers dare not. In the sixties there was an attempt to avoid this discouraging truth.

Those who espoused community action in the sixties located

[18] The policy should be to "raise the lid" on what can be done for the poor, rather than to follow the old "trickle-down" concept. For an essentially nonpolitical, antitechnological approach to the problems of change in our society, see Theodore Roszak, *The Making of a Counter Culture* (New York: Doubleday, 1969). The "flower children" may yet prove to be the most important prophetic minority.

A Conservative Strategy for Social Planning

sources of change within the lower class and defined the problem as the "system." Power was the name of the game. It is now clear that the vast majority of the poor do not wish to change the system; they merely want to be in it. The real force for altering the system lies within the middle-salaried classes, the nonrich, nonpoor, who will be deciding in the seventies whether to live more individualistically or more communally.

Should social planners ignore these groups, they will be doing the poor a disservice. The choice that these groups make will profoundly affect what can be done for the poor. The temptation to regard social change from the tired scenario of the left must be resisted. Change is coming, but it is coming pragmatically. Nothing that can succeed should be ruled out, certainly not simply because it does not fit the canons of a particular political ideology.[19]

For example, one feasible way to increase the effectiveness of social resources and to assure accountability to the public as well as to the consumers is to promote competition among public and private services. A way which deserves exploration is the provision of money or vouchers for the purchase of certain services, giving consumers the opportunity to pick and choose:

> Probably no single development would more enliven and energize the role of government in urban affairs than a move from the *monopoly service* strategy of the grant-in-aid programs to a *market* strategy of providing the most reward to those suppliers that survive competition.[20]

Furthermore, no proposed solution to ghetto problems that is not eventually supported by the majority of the white middle class can possibly succeed:

> The need is to find formulas which would make the new programs as widely acceptable as possible and provide payoffs which would make them tolerable to forces which otherwise would be sure to block them. While such an approach might be resented by citizens already convinced of the need to act drastically in favor of the underclass, the fact is that in a democracy no significant actions can be taken without such political homework.[21]

[19] For a full discussion of this danger, see Michael Walzer, "The Obligations of Oppressed Minorities," *Commentary*, XLIX, No. 5 (1970), 71–80.
[20] Daniel P. Moynihan, "Toward an Urban Policy," *Public Interest*, No. 17 (1969), p. 16.
[21] Amitai Etzoini, quoted in *The Reacting Americans* (New York: American Jewish Committee, 1968), pp. 26–27.

This is not an abandonment of the poor, nor is it the old "trickle-down" concept.

The effect of the nonrich on the poor is too often glossed over by the concern of social workers to be "relevant." As this effect becomes more apparent, advocacy planners of a nonideological bent will find it increasingly difficult to be relevant to all segments of the minority community, let alone the more militant ones—and those planners who are white will find it increasingly difficult to dissent.

The current concern over community control of local institutions and the decentralization of community services is a case in point. Rather than looking upon community control as a necessary shift in the operation of certain ineffective bureaucratic agencies and as a useful training ground for minority leadership, many militants see it as the only problem worthy of consideration. Those who point to the limitations of an overemphasis on community control are branded as racists or enemies of the people. Yet, it is quite clear that the poor cannot be helped solely from a neighborhood base; urban problems cannot really be solved unless attention is given to rural problems as well. So long as there is mass immigration to the cities, economic and social programs aimed at handling many of the problems in the cities will be overwhelmed and undercut. National solutions are in order, as is consideration of the concerns of other groups.

The belief that the lower middle class is satisfied with its life and its prejudices is misguided. It suffers from a sense of lack of respect and dignity. Those who fail to understand this group's attachment to God and country and the desire for material comforts can never mobilize its resources for the common good.[22] The key to effective social planning for all social classes lies in the way that emotional rewards can be derived from proposed programs. The presence or absence of these rewards offers an important clue as to which programs will be opposed or supported.

The "new politics" errs when it suggests that what is required to cure the current civic malaise are simply greater opportunities

---

[22] For a discussion of the effects of loss of social values, see Allen Wheelis, *The Quest for Identity* (New York: W. W. Norton, 1958), pp. 152–73.

A Conservative Strategy for Social Planning

for people to participate in political activity, and the "old politics" errs when it suggests that all people have to do is pay their taxes. Relatively few people of any class can participate in politics or, for that matter, in decision-making of any type, and receive the important rewards of respect and deference through such activity.

The idea that people learn through "dialogues," through discussion of issues, cannot be held by any serious observer of everyday life. The world is not a classroom or a debating society. What is needed is not a "new politics" but a "new citizenship," where opportunities for an assortment of levels and types of participation is available, especially of a nonverbal variety. Dialogues are only meaningful when people have experiences from which they can make judgments about what is said. Simply providing opportunities for democratic talk or decision-making is not enough.

What is *not* being suggested per se is some sort of gigantic self-help campaign or domestic peace corps; rather, the attempt is to point out that rhetoric is not self-actualizing. Merely stating that there is a problem and people should do something is not enough.

For example, unless it is known that 1,000 teen-agers dropped out of high school in 1969, no one can judge how effective are the preventive measures taken in 1970. No one can say whether the concern of an interested citizen for a dropout is more important than would be the presence of another paid teacher in a classroom. But it is certain that people can be interested in lowering the dropout rate, in lessening crime, in matching jobs with people, in lowering the cost of hospital care, if they can judge the effects of their efforts, political or personal. The citizenry has never been seriously involved in solving its problems in such a manner. Short of a crisis, this type of involvement is crucial for mobilizing resources, spiritual and financial.

There are a number of key differences between such a "new citizenship" and past attempts at "voluntarism" in social welfare:

1. Participation would have to be so structured and controlled that all groups and classes were represented. Otherwise, participation can become unevenly stratified, and its humanizing value lost for society as a whole.

2. Involvement would have to be publicly organized and sponsored so that its scope was broad enough not only to attract interest but also to have some chance of success.

3. It would have to be problem-oriented so that the results of paid and voluntary efforts could be gauged. (For example, one would not simply volunteer for work in a settlement house, one would volunteer for work in addiction.) Without such appraisals, involvement can become merely an inadequate substitute for needed funds.

4. It should be focused on only one or two problems at a time so that efforts would not be dissipated and the public could really be kept informed.

5. The new citizenship need not be focused solely on the problems of the poor. Project selection and stimulation is the crucial role of political leadership, whose task it is to provide the citizenry with experiences out of which can grow the sanction for social change, especially for those changes which are beyond the scope of voluntarism.

There are those in social work who would like to be paid a salary to create the revolution in varying degrees. They envisage themselves as part of "the movement," which encompasses groups with a variety of ends and procedures from apolitical, personal, and communal self-fulfillment to radical reform, to nonviolent revolution, to violent revolution. Such practitioners will always be uncomfortable in a profession which has been and will continue to be as much an arm of social stability as of social change.

Social work in America is essentially the creation of people like the French farmer who said that he voted socialist so that there would never be socialism. Nevertheless, because of the injustices in society, it is difficult to resist radical criticism. Honest people with social ideals will also recognize how easy it is to temporize when their own security and status are not threatened.

Should social workers ask the black poor to wait? No one should. Yet the civil rights movement was not started, and could not have been started, by social workers. Other such movements may well be necessary in America. They will not be initiated by

A Conservative Strategy for Social Planning

social workers either, especially those supported by public funds.[23] Only priests are paid salaries, not prophets.

This does not mean that planners should opt out of social action or accept the status quo. Targets have to be picked in the context of a total strategy. Effective social planning for the seventies, which simply means the enactment of programs that give the poor middle-class options, cannot blindly accept just any program, even one that is promulgated by or for the poor. Wars on poverty are not won solely by frontal attacks. If at particular times programs, policies, or procedures such as confrontation won't work, some planners must retain the flexibility to say so.

Older social workers are accused by younger social workers of operating public welfare programs which demean people. While one may agree, it is necessary to point out that the programs mushroomed because of precisely the attitudes and values now espoused by these same young workers: an overly optimistic view of human behavior, more concern with an ideology than with an evaluation of program results, a lack of appreciation of the problems of those not on welfare, and hostility to anything vaguely resembling a contribution for benefits received. Program failures lessen the confidence of the public in planned social change.

Society is now in a crisis situation but has neither the will nor, apparently, the readiness to sanction action. How to create this sanction is a major problem for the seventies. An important consideration is the neutralization of potential opposition to change.

Citizen participation alone will not solve our problems, but an important latent function of citizen involvement, publicly sponsored and coordinated, is the mobilization of a commitment to

[23] There is even a danger to social movements from involvement with social agencies. Cloward and Piven make the point: "If [an agency] means to promote low-income social action, then it must be prepared to support the only effective means open to them—collective protest. It must therefore be prepared to pay a certain price in the form of diminished support from elements in its supporting elitist network. If it is not prepared to pay that price, then such agencies should not impede the development of low-income social movements by supposing that they can intrude upon their autonomy without decisively changing their form and militancy." Richard A. Cloward and Frances F. Piven, "Low-Income People and Political Process" (New York: Mobilization for Youth, 1964; mimeographed), p. 37.

make needed changes. Restricting participation solely to political action or to the problems of one group limits the possibility of change, as it too quickly narrows the base upon which alliances can be built.

The single most important activity for social planners, besides resisting the temptation to become permanent buffers between people and problems, is to make known to the public what it is getting for its time and money so that its faith in its capacity to make a better society is maintained. Great societies are first believed in, then made.

Client, Staff, and the Social Agency

LAWRENCE SHULMAN

THE EMERGENCE OF MILITANT CLIENT GROUPS has focused the attention of our profession on the operations of social agencies. Agencies and social workers are taken to task for failing to meet client needs.

The social worker, in turn, is asked to look at his role in maintaining services which appear to be dysfunctional. He is challenged to change the systems within which he works. His reactions include anger and guilt. On the one hand, he knows that he is not the incompetent that he is made out to be, for many clients have received real help from his agency. On the other hand, many of the charges are echoed by his own unhappiness with agency service and his inability to have impact upon the system. Thus, both for agencies and for the social work profession this is a time of turmoil and anxiety.

However, there is also a great opportunity for change. My optimism flows from the conviction that it is at such difficult times that any formal organization is most amenable to real and permanent change. Kurt Lewin describes systems as maintaining a "quasi-stationary equilibrium"[1] in which "customs" and "social habits" create an "inner resistance" to change. A balance is created so that we can function and not be overwhelmed by chaos. The price paid for this stability is a force which resists demands from the environment to "break the habit" and "unfreeze the custom." Agencies, I believe, follow this rule. The present time of confrontation, with its powerful catharsis of stored-up emotions, can be the additional force needed to free agencies from

[1] Kurt Lewin, "Field Theory in Social Science," in Dorwin Cartwright, ed., *Frontiers in Group Dynamics* (New York: Harper & Row, 1951), p. 224.

their resistance to change and to release the potential for improving service to clients.

It would be naïve, however, to think that the forces which create a readiness for change automatically bring about the changes. Strength for change must come from the system members themselves: clients, social workers, supervisors, and administrators. What is needed is not more rhetoric, but specific help with strategy. We must concentrate on the problems and skills involved in agency change with as much energy as we have devoted to examining our direct work with clients. The agency cannot be regarded as a "given"; it must be an acceptable area of investigation.

THE AGENCY AS A SOCIAL SYSTEM

The complex organism called "agency"[2] consists of two major subsystems: staff members and clients. The client subsystem is further divided into smaller units, such as families, groups, wards, cottages. The staff subsystem is subdivided along functional lines. We have administrators, social workers, supervisors, clerical staff, and so on. In order to analyze a part of a complex system we must set it off with a boundary—an artificial divider which helps focus our attention. In social work, it has been the client subsystem. We study family dynamics, ward behavior, group process, and so forth. While this is necessary, there is the danger that we can take this boundary too seriously. We examine our client interactions as if they were in a "closed" system in which interaction with other subsystems did not have significant impact. For example, we will try to understand the deviant behavior of some hospital patients as *their* problem rather than seeing this behavior as a signal of a problem in hospital care. Or, we will de-

[2] For discussions of organizations and social agencies as social systems see Daniel Katz and Robert L. Kahn, *The Social Psychology of Organizations* (New York: John Wiley & Sons, Inc., 1966); Lawrence Shulman, "Social Systems Theory in Field Instruction: a Case Example," in Gordon Hearn, ed., *The General Systems Approach: Contributions toward an Holistic Conception of Social Work* (New York: Council on Social Work Education, 1969), pp. 37–44; Lawrence Shulman, *A Casebook of Social Work with Groups: the Mediating Model* (New York: Council on Social Work Education, 1969), pp. 201–14; Robert Chin, "The Utility of System Models and Developmental Models for Practitioners," in Warren G. Bennis, Kenneth D. Benne, and Robert Chin, eds., *The Planning of Change* (New York: Holt, Rinehart, and Winston, 1966).

scribe our clients as "unmotivated" when they stop coming to our agencies rather than interpreting their dropping out as "voting with their feet" against poor service.

If we view our agencies as open, dynamic systems, in which each subgroup is somewhat affected by the movements of the other subgroups with which they come in contact, then we cannot isolate our clients as discrete entities. Instead, we must see the total interaction between clients and staff as an essential part of the helping process. In turn, to the degree that staff interactions have a direct impact on the agency service they must also be placed on our agenda. The way in which staff member relations affect the "productivity" of the agency is thus directly connected to issues of client service.

AGENCY MYTH AND AGENCY REALITY

If we are to examine our agencies in a new way we must challenge some of the myths of organizational theory embodied in the thinking of the "scientific management" school of thought which has dominated organizational practice. Two of the universal rules of formal organization emerging from this framework are summarized as follows:

1. *Chain of command:* management's effort to provide a direct system of communication and control. All orders initiate at the top and are filtered down through the links in the management chain until they reach the staff members responsible for their enactment.

2. *Unity of direction:* the principle of unitary effort to move toward the organization's goal. Everyone connected with the organization should be moving in the direction which will fulfill the organizational objectives.[3]

These maxims sound neat, logical, orderly, and suggest a perfectly rational way of running a complex organization. However, troublesome deviations often appear to upset the formal structure. For example, the simple principle of chain of command is

[3] Chris Argyris, "Organizational Leadership," in Luigi Petrullo and Bernand M. Bass, eds., *Leadership and Interpersonal Behavior* (New York: Holt, Rinehart, and Winston, 1961), p. 330.

often frustrated. An agency executive or an administrative group will develop a new form designed to evaluate time demands upon workers in order to improve delivery of service. The form is presented at a staff meeting. Some general questions are asked. There appears to be very little reaction. The form is integrated into the routine procedures of the agency. However, the clerical staff begins to complain about the mistakes that appear on the forms. To some, the errors are just another example of the professional staff's lack of consideration for the clerical workers.

If we consider these mistakes to be simply "unintended consequences," the result of individual deviations, we can shrug them off. The principle of chain of command can remain intact. If, however, we see the agency as a dynamic system, then these "unintended consequences" can be regarded as signals of a larger problem. Let us return to our example of the form and examine it from this second perspective. This time we shall reach behind the ritualized, overt behavior and explore the thoughts and feelings of the actors which were never directly communicated.

Administration: We have this new form which will be helpful in evaluating our services. We will start to implement it next month. Are there any questions?

Professional staff (after asking some routine questions): Well, we will give it a try. (*Real reaction:* Damn! Another piece of paper to fill out—for what purpose? I'm already filling out papers most of the day. They probably don't trust us; this is just another way of spying on our use of time. They treat us like children. They really don't think much of us at all.

Most of this discussion does take place, with much feeling, in the coffee shop after the staff meeting. These reactions and feelings are too strong simply to disappear. They are suppressed and reemerge as indirect, subtle communications to the administration. Forms are late and inaccurate. Simple instructions are misunderstood. Staff members become passive at meetings, or individuals exhibit aggressive behavior. As the late, inaccurate forms are received by the clerical staff, their communication back to the workers often takes the following form:

Clerical staff (usually expressed in a memo): Client contact forms have been coming in late. Could you make some effort to have them

Client, Staff, and the Social Agency 25

in by the first of the month? Or: Miss Smith, you appear to misunderstand the procedure for filling in form number 17. It is as follows . . . (*Real reaction:* College education! My God, they're all a bunch of illiterates. Don't they realize how much I have to do? I'll teach them. Let them wait a few more weeks for their process recordings.)

Meanwhile, back at the coffee shop, one social worker turns to the others and comments on the inefficiency of the clerical staff—they are a full three weeks behind in typing the records. Also, the administration has just issued a memo urging the staff to catch up on their statistics.

I maintain that this example is not unique but, rather, characteristic of agency staff interaction. Since staff members are involved in "a collaboration on the business of the agency,"[4] this example reveals some obstacles which may emerge to frustrate attempts to carry out agency business.

Communication. Open communication between staff members is hard to achieve. I have written elsewhere of the barriers to communication within small groups.[5] I think they can be found in an agency culture as well. For example, taboos are created by a general consensus to block or prohibit discussion in areas of sensitivity and deep concern. Feelings which may be painful and frightening to workers may be suppressed by defenses which safeguard them from their real or imagined potency. Even when staff members are fully conscious of their feelings, open expression is blocked by a fear of their impact on colleagues and persons in authority. It takes all of the administrator's skill to create a staff culture which encourages the direct expression of hidden negatives, anger and hurt. Instead, staff members are often given double messages in which they are invited to "say what's on their mind," and then promptly chastised when they accept the invitation.

Client-staff communication is often blocked by the same barriers. The consumers of service, who are in an excellent position to evaluate its impact and provide necessary feedback, are cut off

[4] William Schwartz, "Group Work in Public Welfare," *Public Welfare*, XXVI, No. 4 (1968), 333.
[5] Lawrence Shulman, "Social Work Skill: the Anatomy of a Helping Act," in *Social Work Practice, 1969* (New York: Columbia University Press, 1969), pp. 29–48.

from making this essential contribution. I suspect that problems in open communication between staff levels help to close staff to direct feedback from clients. They will not reach for or accept negatives if they have no place to go with them.

Communication problems are not limited to difficulties between levels of authority. Just as clients must struggle to be honest with each other in their efforts at mutual aid, staff members are affected by years of exposure to artificial rules of behavior which serve to impede their efforts to work with each other.

Chris Argyris [6] describes how the formal organization stresses "cognitive reality" as opposed to expressions of real feeling, unilateral control in human relations, and the artificial separation of "process and task." He points out that this leads to restriction of: genuine interpersonal feedback; openness to new ideas, feelings, and values; owning to one's own views and tolerating others; experimenting and risk-taking—all factors which vitally affect the productivity of an organization.[7]

The illusion of work. Agency staff will not directly admit to the existence of a problem in their way of working. It will be covered up to create the impression that there is no problem. "Pseudo effectiveness," "artificial order," and "the illusion of work" are all phrases which describe how "organizational ineffectiveness" can be ignored. In industry, advancing technology helps to conceal organizational problems. In social work agencies, where the "product" of our work is less tangible, there is even less open evidence of our mistakes. It was nicely said by an experienced caseworker who was learning to work with groups in

---

[6] Chris Argyris, *Integrating the Individual and the Organization* (New York: John Wiley & Sons, Inc., 1964).

[7] The business world and an increasing number of social work agencies have taken note of the problems of authentic communication in staff relations. One method of change, *T*-groups, is drawn from the "sensitivity training" movement. It has been my observation that "open communication" through such efforts does not have real impact on the agency system. The *T*-group remains an island within the agency with little transfer to everyday operations. An intensive study by Blake and Mouton revealed that "additional attributes of organizational change performance failed to show significant change associated with training." See Robert R. Blake and Jane S. Mouton, "Organization Change through the Process Training Hypotheses," Seminar on Organization Change, University of California, 1963; mimeographed.

Client, Staff, and the Social Agency

a seminar. Fear of moving from individual work to group work had emerged:

I asked them what it was that was different about working with groups—why the special fear. Louise laughed and said, "When I work with a client and he doesn't return after the second visit I can chalk it up to resistance and close the file, but if ten group members don't come back, where am I?"

This safety valve, the externalizing of a problem in the helping relationship, offers a way to continue working without attacking our more difficult problems. A "quasi equilibrium" is maintained, and the critical feedback from staff and clients that is essential for agency renewal is stifled. The notion of the "good agency," one without problems, one that can avoid conflicts, is held up as the goal. The myth of agency infallibility prevents staff from developing constructive adaptive behavior.

Staff members trapped by the "illusion of work" often adopt one of the following strategies:

1. They may openly go along with administrative or peer group decisions and then use passive resistance, as in the example of the forms, to express their true feelings.

2. They may attempt open resistance, which usually identifies them as "deviants" in the system. The system will allow a degree of deviance—in fact, needs and maintains it—but if the staff member exceeds certain boundaries (a form of acting out), he will be forced out of the agency.

3. They may search out ways to circumvent the restraining policies and attempt to provide a particular service in spite of the agency.[8]

4. They may leave the agency for what they hope will be a better situation. Often, such a move is embellished by the worker's farewell to the administration in which he finally says what he wanted to say all along.

5. They may attempt to work out an effective strategy for influencing agency change.

Organizational emotionality. "Illogical" behavior in agencies

[8] For an example of this strategy see Archie Hanlan, "Counteracting Problems of Bureaucracy in Public Welfare," *Social Work*, XII, No. 3 (1967), 88–94.

seems illogical *only* because we assume that all staff members are actually working on the business of the agency. If, instead, we assume that they may be working on *their way of working together,* then the organizational behavior themes emerge with clarity and a new logic. Apparently counterproductive behavior takes on new meaning, becoming, consciously or unconsciously, indirect communication about urgent system maintenance problems.

In describing organizational behavior in this way I am extending some of our hypotheses about small group behavior to larger systems. Although analogies between small and large systems do not always hold, our experience with "micro-societies" can reveal promising insights. Bion,[9] for example, has developed a "work-emotionality" theory of groups, explaining group behavior as a result of the conflict between efforts to work on the group's "task" and efforts to deal with the "emotions" generated by the work. For example, some forms of "irrational" group behavior can be understood if viewed as if the group were working on its feelings of dependency toward the group leader and not on its immediate task.

I propose that this may be a helpful model for examining agency systems. In their efforts to work productively, staff in subgroups and staff as a whole will be affected by the generation of feelings, both positive and negative. The emotionality of the organization can lead to maladaptive patterns of behavior. We have seen how the myth of the organizational rationality dominates our thinking, and that the expression of feeling is generally suppressed. It could help to explain many of the deviations in organizational behavior if emotionality were given a central place in our model.

To take things further, I shall borrow a notion from Schwartz's [10] analysis of small groups and suggest that at any one time the organization as a whole or its subgroups will be working either on its tasks as an agency (providing client service) or on

[9] W. R. Bion, *Experiences in Groups* (New York: Basic Books, 1965).
[10] William Schwartz, "On the Use of Groups in Social Work Practice," in William Schwartz and Serapio Zalba, eds., *The Practice of Group Work* (New York: Columbia University Press, 1970), pp. 3-24.

its way of working. In addition, work on the way of working may be subdivided into the "intimacy theme" (the interactional system of peers) or the "authority theme" (the interactional system of superiors and subordinates). In our example of the new form, conflict between clerical staff and workers would be described as the "intimacy theme" while conflict between the workers and the administration would be the "authority theme."

Problems in the way of working will draw energy away from the tasks of the agency and result in diminishing effectiveness. A major complexity in understanding agency functioning, therefore, is the difficulty in understanding the specific task being worked on at any one moment. Obviously, the agency system needs the help of all involved, staff and clients, if it is to function well and renew itself.

PROFESSIONAL IMPACT ON THE AGENCY SYSTEM

Staff members can help to "hedge against the system's own complexity,"[11] and there are various roles in which staff members have system impact:

1. Workers who deal directly with clients occupy a critical position at the point of contact between agency service and client need. Although low in the hierarchy, they have a functionally critical role. They are analogous to nerve endings for the agency organism, for they are closest to the signals of client feedback.

2. Middle-range supervisors occupy similar positions in relation to workers. The place they occupy, often described as being "caught in the middle," may be transformed into a strategic location for agency impact.

3. The agency executive, more than any other staff member, can influence the "culture" of the agency and create conditions for system change. He can bring agency, staff, and clients into more direct contact with the community. Finally, in addition to functions emerging from his professional role as worker, supervisor, and so on, each staff member is a colleague or subordinate.

---

[11] William Schwartz, "Private Troubles and Public Issues: One Social Work Job or Two?" in *The Social Welfare Forum, 1969* (New York: Columbia University Press, 1969), p. 40.

In his daily functioning he has impact on the agency's operations.

The worker. My description of the worker, standing between the agency and the client, implies a special role. One social work theoretician who has incorporated a "third-force" notion into his theory is William Schwartz. He has developed a generic practice theory called the "mediating model." [12] The theory's central assumption is that of a "symbiotic" relationship between interdependent systems. For the client-agency relationship Schwartz recognizes the existence of "quarrels" and "nasty feelings" but he maintains that

> the fact remains that the basic relationship between an institution and its people is symbiotic; each needs the other for his own survival. Each individual needs to negotiate the systems with which he must come to terms—school, welfare, occupation, neighborhood, and others. Each agency, on its part, needs to justify its existence by serving the people for whom it was designed. It is a form of social contract; and when the arrangement goes wrong, as it frequently does, those who claim that the contract is broken do no service to the people or to the agency. The arena of need remains the same, and the symbiosis remains intact—merely obscure to the unpracticed eye.[13]

The social worker, in Schwartz's scheme, would assume a "buffer" position and mediate the engagement when the symbiosis was blocked. One task would be to help clients individually or in groups to deal with the agency system. A second task would be to work directly with the staff system:

> ... the worker feeds in his direct experience with the struggles of his clients, searches out the staff stake in reaching and innovating, and brings administration wherever possible into direct contact with clients who are seeking new ways of being served.[14]

Work with the staff system is a distinctive feature of this model since it assumes that staff members are concerned people with complex tasks, in ambivalent agencies, needing all the help they can get. It asks the worker, as part of his professional function, to use his skill with system representatives as well as with clients. He must listen, reach for hidden negatives, tolerate deviancy, de-

---

[12] William Schwartz, "The Social Worker in the Group," in *The Social Welfare Forum* (New York: Columbia University Press, 1969).

[13] Schwartz, "Private Troubles . . . ," p. 38.   [14] *Ibid.* pp. 41–42.

velop strategies; in short, use all his skills. The demand for skill is great because, as one worker points out, "hell hath no fury like a helping system scorned." [15]

This is not an easy task for the worker. Skills in working with the system, although similar to those used in working with clients, have to be relearned through practice. If a worker is not working in a system with an open culture, one that encourages this "third-force" role, then he must risk himself from a vulnerable position. This creates anxiety in the worker, and his own feelings may become an obstacle to his effective functioning.

Observation of beginning efforts at systems work reveals certain characteristic patterns of action. First, the worker proceeds as if the engagement were between himself and the agency. He responds to the first offerings of dissatisfaction by identifying with the clients' concerns and attempting to exhort them to confront the system immediately. In his haste to act, he misses indirect clues which reveal the clients' ambivalence, fears, and feelings of impotence. Perhaps, because these feelings come close to many of his own, he does not help clients deal with them in preparation for taking on a complex task. He also ignores work with the system representatives which might help prepare them for the engagement and instead proceeds into battle. When the confrontation takes place, if it does, he finds passive clients, ill-prepared to carry out the worker's strategy—one they never actually owned. The encounter is lifeless, one-sided, and the worker feels impelled to take over the client's task—an action that cuts him off from the staff system representatives as a source of aid. He later explains his action by commenting that his clients were "not ready." He is out of touch with his clients' ambivalence and has, in effect, used them in his efforts to affect the system. He has denied their strength, and his efforts will be fruitless.

A second pattern can be identified, in which the worker makes an initial effort to reach system representatives and receives a cold response. Supervisors acknowledge the problem but feel that nothing can be done. Administrators respond to the worker with

[15] Lyn Hoffman and Lorence Long, "A Systems Dilemma," *Family Process,* VIII (1969), 231.

direct or indirect hostility, communicating a "don't-rock-the-boat" message. Skilled workers, who understand resistance, who tolerate deviancy, and who deal with client hostility, retreat at the first sign of similar reactions by staff members. Their comments reveal insights into the dynamics of the interaction: "The executive *should* be responsive to change; he *should* be different. These people are social workers, they *should* listen; they are *supposed* to care. They are not interested in what I have to say. It's hopeless." The worker feels hurt and let down by his supervisor, by the administrator, and even by his colleagues. They have revealed themselves to be human, with frailty, thin skins, and ambivalence. The worker, counting on their strength to help him in his complex tasks, instead finds weaknesses. It is a profound discovery, and I suspect that the worker never forgives them or gives them a second chance. He joins them in an unstated agreement that he will not try again.

Finally, this apparent block to systems change leads the worker to develop patterns of work with clients, which "cool them off." When early signals of dissatisfaction emerge, the worker listens, allows the clients to "ventilate," acknowledges the problem, and then asks them to "get back to work." Doing something about the problem is not included as part of the work. There are theories which support the notion that complaining about the agency is simply a way of avoiding the "real work," and at times this may be true. The worker does not let the clients stay with their thoughts, which may lead to doing something about the agency. He is blocked by his personal view of what lies at the end of the path and by a staff system which he perceives as unresponsive to him and to the clients. Once again, feelings go underground, only to haunt the work in indirect ways which are not always understood by clients or worker.

With the client-agency mediation process so complex, skill development is critical. These skills include openness to client negatives, sensitivity to the ambivalence of both the client and the agency system, a willingness to stay with client and staff work in the face of resistance, and, most important, an ability to see both the agency's and the client's stake in the engagement, even when both sides have lost sight of it.

The worker in this model is not trying to smooth over issues or create conflicts. He is trying to bring into the open problems in which service and need are not connecting, problems that both agency staff and clients have a stake in resolving. His activities will inevitably be disruptive because they are designed to challenge the false sense of order that is a major obstacle to agency renewal. The work between agency and clients will be difficult for both as real feelings emerge, but the worker must retain his faith in the inherent capacity of the engagement to succeed.[16]

The supervisor. The supervisor is in essentially the same position as the worker. His task is to help staff members carry out the work of the agency. In work with staff groups, he faces the same dynamics that are found in work with clients. I believe we can apply the mediation theory to the function of the supervisor.

We can begin by clarifying the "symbiosis" or "common ground" between staff members and administration. Schwartz points out:

The staff meeting is neither a social occasion or a therapeutic enterprise, but a collaboration on the business of the agency. Further, it is a collaboration in which the administration and staff have certain (not all) interests in common, however obscured these may sometimes be: administration is charged with maintaining and improving the service of the agency, which depends in turn on high staff morale and the steady improvement of practitioner skill; staff members, on their part, want to feel competent, that they are working for a "good agency," that they have a contribution to make and that they can get help in making it.[17]

The supervisor, in this model, carries out his "third-force" role between administration and staff. His tasks include direct work with his subordinates to strengthen them as a mutual aid system and work with administrative representatives. Following are some

[16] For examples of social work system intervention see *ibid.;* Stanley J. Sterling, "Organizational Change and Social Group Work Practice" (New York: Columbia University School of Social Work; mimeographed); Morris S. Schwartz and Gwen Tudor Will, "Intervention and Change on a Mental Hospital Ward," in Bennis, Benne, and Chin, *op. cit.,* pp. 564–82; Zelda P. Leader Foster, "How Social Work Can Influence Hospital Management of Fatal Illness," *Social Work,* X, No. 4 (1965), 30–35; Hyman J. Weiner, "Toward Techniques for Social Change," *Social Work,* VI, No. 2 (1961), 26–35; Lawrence Shulman, *A Casebook of Social Work with Groups.* . . .

[17] William Schwartz, "Group Work in Public Welfare," *Public Welfare,* XXVI, No. 4 (1968), 333.

examples of work with staff groups which illustrate the function. The excerpts are drawn from the records of supervisors in a state public welfare agency who were training in the use of group methods for staff management.

In the first excerpt an administrative supervisor opens a meeting designed to examine the agency's evaluation procedure. Her group consists of middle-range supervisors. She begins by listening to the chatter which precedes the meeting and noting potentially significant themes of discussion. She then makes a brief opening statement which clarifies the purpose of the session, acknowledges the difficulties involved, and points out the areas of common ground:

Prior to the meeting, a newly appointed supervisor expressed her frustration in evaluating caseworkers who had been on a peer relationship with her prior to her present position. Her expressed inadequacies received concurrence as other supervisors joined the discussion. Resistance to evaluation developed as a subtheme as the group assembled.

I started the meeting by expressing my appreciation of their difficult position in an evaluation process, and suggested that we use this session to discuss the problems of evaluation and help each other in devising a better evaluation procedure. I stated that I felt that the administration and supervisors had a common stake in evaluation since we could not otherwise objectively deal with caseworker performance. I further suggested that the caseworkers have a vital interest in evaluation since otherwise they do not know how they stand in relation to the job.

The next excerpt reveals a supervisor reaching past the ritualistic positive evaluation of a training program for new workers to encourage the expression of negative feelings:

I mentioned that we had one half hour left. I said I would like to use half of it for an oral evaluation of orientation and then they could have the other fifteen minutes to complete their written evaluation. This was their last session. How had orientation seemed to them? They mentioned that it had been helpful and made several other positive comments. I wondered if it had all been this positive, to which several of them brought up and discussed some of the more boring parts. I mentioned that as a group they were quite different. Several of the leaders had commented on this to me. They had been unusually quiet and had not responded much with discussion and questions. Did they feel this was true and if so why? Several of the group responded, and

Client, Staff, and the Social Agency

the consensus was that several of them had had social work experience in other agencies and they felt the orientation program was geared below them. Two of the workers who had no previous experience said they had not said much as they were busy absorbing the information and feeling slightly overwhelmed. One of the group members suggested they go around the circle and comment on their amount of participation and why. The rest of the group agreed, and their answers mainly fell into the above two areas.

In the final set of excerpts a supervisor calls a unit meeting in order to share information concerning agency changes. The meeting takes place the day after pay checks containing a disappointing annual raise have been distributed. The low salary paid to welfare workers contributes to their poor morale and reinforces the low estimate that workers have of their ability. In the early part of the meeting the negative feelings emerge, but the supervisor defensively cuts them off with a "someone up there is working on the problem" comment.

Before the meeting started Mrs. Dory asked about the salary increments that were included in the pay check they received yesterday. There were comments of "Yeah," from two other workers present at that time. At that point, Mrs. Lawrence walked in, and I said that our opening question was in reference to increments. I told her this was only the routine annual increment and that it was hopeful that higher salaries would be forthcoming in a few months. At that point there were no further questions about the raises. I told the group that I had called them together to present information regarding procedures we should initiate in the Intake Unit.

As the supervisor focuses on her agenda the workers go along halfheartedly. Their discussion is rambling and unproductive. The theme of being unappreciated emerges again in a new form. There is a conflict between the "set-up" task of the group and the "real" task. Their strong feelings about the salary increases force the issue back to the surface:

Mr. Dean said, emphatically, that they are always doing things which take up the little time they have—there is a class next week which will knock out a half a day. Mrs. Lawrence mentioned a group workshop she had to go to for another half day. Mrs. Wilson said to Mr. Dean that the Welfare Board was giving Friday or Monday off as a bonus day for the hard work the staff had put in. She continued that the

Board was giving this day off instead of their "lousy salary increase." Mr. Dean and the other caseworkers did not seem impressed. They all said they could not afford to take the day off, and if they did they would have to work harder on Tuesday, Wednesday, Thursday, and Friday.

The supervisor responds by closing off their discussion with a supporting comment on the day-off policy. The meeting continues with oscillation between the set tasks, and their unhappiness.

I said the idea was that they would have a better outlook on their work if they had the additional day's rest or freedom from the job, and had a long weekend before they had to face their chores again. I sensed that there wasn't a great deal of agreement with my statement. Before any length of silence or before any other sign of their dissatisfaction cropped up, Mrs. Wilson said their feeling was that there must be some way we could speed up the time between an applicant's completion of the application and the receipt of his check. There was much discussion on alternative means of issuing the grants. However, it was realized at the end of the conversation, there seemed to be little alternative.

At this point in the meeting the supervisor begins to operate in a more skillful manner. First, she recognizes her mistake even as she is making it by acknowledging to herself that the meeting is not going well. Second, she reads Mr. Dean's nonverbal signals as an indirect communication and responds to them directly. Third, she recognizes that Mr. Dean's "deviancy" may be a signal of how the whole group feels about the work of the session:

At this point, the group leader noticed, as she had several times, Mr. Dean's yawning. Although he seemed attentive during discussions, and attempted to contribute, he stretched, squirmed, and yawned from time to time, which were obvious signals. I asked him if he were that tired, or bored, or what. Mr. Dean said that he was not asleep, just depressed. Mrs. Wilson said that it seems that the whole team is demoralized. The whole thing boils down to their concern about their salaries.

The supervisor next acknowledges their feelings and recognizes the way in which they are obstructing the work of the group. She asks the group members to work on their real concern:

I commented that I really could empathize with them because I had reservations about the situation myself. I wondered what the solution could be because it was obvious that we were in varying degrees of unhappiness, and that we weren't going to do our jobs.

Mrs. Wilson said that we needed about half an hour for all the employees to meet together, not to be reprimanded or punished but in an environment conducive to the expression of their feelings. She wished the Directress could be absent from the meeting. She then quickly countered her statement by saying that the meeting would be of no value if she didn't sit there and hear the feelings of the staff.

As the group members begin to work on how to deal with the agency system, Mrs. Wilson's comments reveal their concern about talking directly with the Directress. The supervisor returned to this theme at a later time in preparation for a scheduled staff meeting. At this point, she offers to bring the feelings of the staff members to the attention of the administration:

I said that I would be willing to discuss with the Directress and the other supervisors the consensus of the group that a free staff meeting should be held in order to discuss their situation. I said I had to dictate process records of this meeting for my group work workshop. I could show her my record to let her know the discontent of the staff members. The four group members thought this was a good idea. I said I would let them know the outcome of my discussion and that, hopefully, we could set up a staff meeting within the next couple of weeks.

These excerpts illustrate the way in which feelings can obstruct the work of a staff group and the skills required to deal with them. This was the beginning of a process which involved a full staff meeting and meetings of the Welfare Board. The work that followed was complex, difficult, and only partially successful. Some movement was made, however, because the staff group was supported by the supervisor in working on its task of negotiating the agency environment.

The executive. While some of the functions of the executive are peculiar to his special responsibilities, such as hiring staff, formulating budgets, and so forth, a major part of his function can be described in the same terms I have used in dealing with the worker and the supervisor. The executive is the principal catalyst in helping the staff system develop an open culture for work. His central role multiplies his impact on the staff system, and his skillful work can free staff to risk in carrying out their functions. Lack of skill on his part, in turn, will pose tremendous obstacles to the work of the agency. Staff meetings, for example, require as much skill in group leadership as is demanded of workers with client counseling groups.

In addition to mediating between various parts of his staff system, the director finds himself at the boundary between agency and community. Garfield describes his function:

> Another task is to mediate between the service he has helped to initiate, and the board to whom he is accountable. More specifically, just as the social work practitioner takes his cues from the problems of clients and seeks to help them negotiate their environment, the social work executive takes his cues from the evidence of the service and brings this to the board's attention; he does so through written records and reports and, above all, through arranging face-to-face encounters among board, staff and clientele. In this way he creates the opportunity for the board to confront the evidence of the service it has authorized, and obligates the board to decide on courses of action. In sum, he challenges and frees the board to come to terms with the demands of its work, including the advocacy of the public issues made evident and urgent in the service.[18]

The staff member. In addition to his professional role in which the work and the skills required emerge from his professional function, each staff person is also a member of the staff system. In his role he is called upon to interact with other staff members at staff meetings, conferences, and case discussions. His activities will flow from his function as member, colleague, co-worker, and so on. He has no special function as a worker in this role. In his role as worker, he acted to help others act. Now, he tries to influence the direction of the work toward his own notions of agency effectiveness. He risks his own ideas, listens to others, challenges what he perceives as unclear thinking, shares his feelings about the work, listens to the feelings of others; in short, he tries to harness the other staff members to his notion of urgency and to convince them of his own view of how the work should proceed.

[18] Goodwin Garfield, "Social Work as Mutual Aid: an Administrative View," National Conference on Social Welfare, 1969, pp. 26-27; Abraham Zaleznik, "Managerial Behavior and Interpersonal Competence," *Behavioral Science,* IX (1964), 156-66.

Work between staff members is not a polite tea party in which each colleague tries to "out-social-work" the others. When it is going well it is argumentative, risky, open, honest, and deals with real issues and feelings. It is out of the debate, a conflict of views, that a synthesis emerges. Our experience should show us that the danger lies not in the risk of abrasiveness but rather in the quicksand of artificial agreement. To the degree that supervisors and executives carry out their professional functions with staff groups, this manner of work will be encouraged; in fact, demanded. Once staff groups learn to work this way, they will not quickly abandon it.

The skills of the member do not flow from the functional assignment as social worker but rather from the productivity requirements of the staff group. Member behavior and the nature of the work constitute a relatively unexplored area which may yield important insights. Each one of us must find his unique way of functioning. However, a deeper understanding of this area may help us make more effective contributions while allowing us to maintain our essential personal integrity. This can be particularly important when a worker seeks to have impact on a system in which those with responsibility for the maintenance of the system's productivity are not skillful.

My description of the agency culture only begins to reveal the complexity of organizational process. Any client, worker, supervisor, or executive knows the depth of feeling evoked by his efforts at negotiating within complex agency systems.

What is needed, I believe, is a focus on systems work as an essential area for study. Workers, supervisors, and executives must try different strategies and record, in process, the results of their efforts. The mediating theory offers a promising model for practice with clients and staff. It needs to be tested, and the results should be made available for professional scrutiny. Other theorists, suggesting other models for systems work, have the same obligation to test their theories in the crucible of practice and to share the results. We need to see what these models look like in action, through recording of some form, in order to evaluate the process as well as the proponent's conclusions.

In addition, we need to build into schools of social work a focus on systems work which captures and mobilizes student disenchantment with field practice agencies. Students need to theorize about their agency systems in the classroom. Field supervisors must help students develop skill in dealing with their agencies. Process recording and line-by-line analysis of practice should be used in staff work as well as in client contacts.

In my practice class, analysis of systems work is included as an area for investigation. In one of the last few sessions of a second-year class, although the class had agreed to move into this area, the discussion was not going well, and I pointed this out. With a great deal of anger in her voice, Gwen agreed with me: they were stuck because of how they felt. She said: "I don't want to be like the staff people I see in the agencies now, who are passive and go along with everything, but I'm afraid of making trouble. I'm angry that I'm going to be put into a position where I have to feel threatened and upset and have to have all kinds of demands made on me to be so skillful."

Gwen and the other students were afraid of being like the staff members they saw. What they need to discover is that these staff members do not want to be that way either.

From Social Work to Social Administration

ARCHIE HANLAN

"Activism" is a term that has enjoyed popular usage since, a few years ago, California college students wore necklaces of mutilated IBM cards and protested an administration that they regarded as unresponsive, alienating, and sometimes even brutal. These students were the advance guard of a new militancy, an activist orientation on the part of some college students and young professionals. In recent years they have been joined by such diverse groups as organized tenants, welfare recipients, and welfare workers who consider computerized welfare budgets and welfare directors to be symbols of the steel-hearted administrators who do the dirty work of our society.[1]

The increasing protest and demonstration against the administration of our social welfare agencies are only part of a larger debate in this country. Administrators of all the agencies and organizations of society have been characterized as members of an elite class in a class-torn system. They are portrayed as symbols of authority who are implacable in the face of our pervasive social needs and problems. In one of the more flamboyant descriptions of twentieth-century man, he is described as psychologically and economically split asunder by the "Omnipotent Administrators" who rule over the "Supermasculine Menials."[2] Thus, the rhetoric on administration is a curious mixture of psychological, eco-

[1] For accounts of the organization of welfare recipients and workers, see Joseph E. Paull, "Recipients Aroused: the New Welfare Rights Movement," *Social Work*, XII, No. 2 (1967), 101–6; Lee Rainwater, "The Revolt of the Dirty-Workers," *Trans-action*, V, No. 1 (1967), 2, 64. For a broader view of recent protest movements, see Jerome H. Skolnick, *The Politics of Protest* (New York: Ballantine Books, 1969).

[2] Eldridge Cleaver, *Soul on Ice* (New York: Dell Publishing Co., 1968), pp. 179–80.

nomic, and sociological arguments. In social welfare and elsewhere, we can no longer wish away or dismiss the arguments simply because they are rhetorical.

These emotionally charged views of administration make it difficult to discuss the subject, and even in the profession of social work, "administration" has become an obscene fourteen-letter word. It is argued that the executive constrains the development of the autonomous practitioner. He is the captive of elitist power groups in the community. He is punitive, self-interested, and, worse yet, an anal-compulsive personality who imposes his will on a powerless clientele. The ghosts of Freud, Marx, and Weber are invoked: we are confronted by unresolvable Oedipal conflicts, inevitable class struggles, and uncontrollable bureaucracies.[3]

Yet all of these dialectical dilemmas obscure crucial administrative goals and interventions for achieving the needed social changes in our society. We will not humanize our social agencies and institutions by bromides or by random, irrational behavior. It is only through some reasoned and rational explication of social change, by debureaucratizing our organizations, and by demonstrably effective strategies for achieving the desired changes, that we may lead ourselves to something other than an apocalyptic end to our recurring social crises.

An initial step for social work, then, is to strain toward some conceptual clarity when ambiguity and distortion exist. Our literature and research suggest that there are at least three models of administration in the education and practice of social workers. These models are not separate and mutually exclusive entities; rather, they represent an overlapping continuum of theories, knowledge, and skills. Yet some important distinctions can be made among them in terms of their differing emphases on assumptions, goals, and interventions. And these distinctions are

---

[3] These dialectical conflicts are embraced in the writings of Marcuse and discussed by George Kateb, "The Political Thought of Herbert Marcuse," *Commentary*, XLIX, No. 1 (1970), 48–63. For an incisive comment on social work's misuse of the theories of Marx and Weber, see S. K. Khinduka, "Community Development: Potentials and Limitations," in *Social Work Practice, 1969* (New York: Columbia University Press, 1969), p. 18.

Social Work to Social Administration

significantly related to the way in which we perceive the social work profession in relation to the larger society.

This continuum of administration in social work will be divided into three segments: (1) social work administration; (2) social welfare administration; and (3) social administration. These three represent a broad spectrum of perspectives and activities within the profession which range from micro- to macro-emphases on the human being and his environment. The three models will be explicated in terms of their assumptions, goals, and interventions.

SOCIAL WORK ADMINISTRATION

Perhaps the largest percentage of social workers employ the social work administration model. For example, a recent survey of members of the National Association of Social Workers (NASW) was concerned with the primary job functions of social workers. Almost half of the respondents (49.7 percent reported that administration is their primary job function.[4] Only one third (33.4 percent) reported casework as their primary job function; 2 percent, community organization; and one percent, group work. Given the method focus of our practice, and the NASW's exclusion of administration from that practice,[5] what is the knowledge and skill base for this large body of social workers whose major function is administration?

Presumably, the answer lies in the term "social work administration," which most frequently has referred to the method approach.[6] That is, it has generally referred to a combination of the knowledge and skills of one or more of the three methods, applied

---

[4] Alfred M. Stamm, "NASW Membership: Characteristics, Deployment, and Salaries," *Personnel Information, NASW*, XII, No. 3 (1969), 39.

[5] For the working definition of social work, see Harriett M. Bartlett, "Toward Clarification and Improvement of Social Work Practice," *Social Work*, III, No. 2 (1958), 3–8.

[6] Although the working definition of social work practice excludes administration from practice, other social workers have strained to define social work administration as a full partner in professional practice. For example, see E. Elizabeth Glover, "Social Welfare Administration: a Social Work Method," *Child Welfare*, XLIV (1965), 431–39. Heffernan suggests that many of the professional issues are

by the social work administrator. Rather than articulating new knowledge and skills, the emphasis is upon some synthesis of methods in the interventions employed by social workers in administrative positions.

This model of administration is logically related to the career patterns of many social work executives. In other words, the directors of many casework agencies have moved from caseworker to supervisor to administrator. Group work agencies are most frequently administered by group workers, and this small group of practitioners has produced a large portion of the social work texts on administration.[7] Health and welfare councils and planning agencies tend to draw their executives from social workers who have had community organization training, and some recent social work literature links administration with community organization.[8]

Basic assumptions for social work administration derive, then, from the assumptions inherent in our three methods. Each method has implied a distinct social work body of knowledge and skills, and this assumption logically holds for social work administration. Thus, the knowledge base for social work administration is to be found primarily in the substantive areas of social work, not in other disciplines.

Interventions generated by social work administration follow the methods approach. There is particular emphasis on use of clinical skills in individual and group interpersonal relations among employees. These skills are compatible with the human

---

far from resolved: W. Joseph Heffernan, Jr., "Some Dysfunctions in the Teaching of Administration in Schools of Social Work," in Heffernan and Sue Spencer, eds., *Education of the Welfare Administrator* (Nashville, Tenn.: University of Tennessee School of Social Work, 1967; mimeographed), pp. 14–20.

[7] For example, Harleigh B. Trecker, *Group Process in Administration* (New York: Woman's Press, 1950); Arthur L. Swift, Jr., *Make Your Agency More Effective* (New York: Association Press, 1941). For administration as a combination of casework, group work, and "the emerging principles of administration," see Ray Johns, *Executive Responsibility* (New York: Association Press, 1954), p. 26.

[8] See Arnold Gurin, "The Community Organization Curriculum Development Project: a Preliminary Report," *Social Service Review*, XLII (1968), 421–34. For an overlapping of administration with community organization, see the "social planning model" in Jack Rothman, "Three Models of Community Organization Practice," in *Social Work Practice, 1968* (New York: Columbia University Press, 1968), pp. 16–47.

relations approach in management literature, with growing interest in administrative use of sensitivity training, and with an emphasis on leadership styles and behavior.[9] Given a dominance of the casework method in social work, it is reasonable to expect reliance on clinical skills as the social worker moves into administration.

The assumptions underlying our practice are closely intertwined with the major goals of the profession, and the goals for social work administration are clearly within the broad social work goal of enhancement of social functioning.[10] Drawing upon more specific goals suggested by Rosen and Connaway, social work administration is clearly compatible with these purposes of the profession: providing and distributing societal resources and helping persons to use maximally the social resources available to them.[11] With emphasis upon existing goods and services, existing programs and agencies, these purposes are essentially residual social welfare functions.[12] Within this context, this model of social work administration is well within the mainstream of social work practice.

SOCIAL WELFARE ADMINISTRATION

Social welfare administration is distinguished from social work administration in terms of the degree of emphasis rather than in absolute differences. The term has been used to stress the relevance of social science knowledge in the management of human service organizations.[13] While this point of view does not

[9] The human relations approach is summarized in Daniel Katz and Robert L. Kahn, *The Social Psychology of Organizations* (New York: John Wiley & Sons, Inc., 1966), pp. 396–425.
[10] Werner W. Boehm, "The Nature of Social Work," *Social Work*, III, No. 2 (1958), 10–18.
[11] Aaron Rosen and Ronda S. Connaway, "Public Welfare, Social Work, and Social Work Education," *Social Work*, XIV, No. 2 (1969), 91–92.
[12] In a similar context, it has been noted that the residual aspects of social work generate a "preoccupation with process and with personality that keeps community development from becoming an effective instrument for large-scale institutional change" (Khinduka, *op. cit.*, p. 25). The distinctions between residual and institutional functions are drawn in Harold L. Wilensky and Charles N. Lebeaux, *Industrial Society and Social Welfare* (New York: Free Press, 1965), pp. 138–40.
[13] Sarri contrasts social welfare administration with some dysfunctions in the social work method approach to administration. See Rosemary Sarri, "Education for

necessarily deny the knowledge and skills base of the three social work methods, it does place those methods in a broader context of knowledge which social workers need for the administration of social welfare programs and agencies.[14] On the continuum, this model may be seen as moving away from a central concern with indigenous social work knowledge and away from a major focus on individual and group behavior. Instead, it moves toward a critical and differential extrapolation of existing and developing social science knowledge in the areas of social welfare policy and administration.

The assumptions which pertain here derive from more than an internal perspective of social work. Rather than accepting some prior definitions of methods and practice in social work, this model assumes that it is the interface between social work and social science knowledge which is important, and a central task is to apply the social science knowledge to goals and tasks of the profession. The model does not require clinical skills.

Interventions generated by social welfare administration are related more to social science-management tasks than to any one of the social work methods. Thus, components of the decision-making process become a series of interrelated activities and interventions for the administrator.[15] Priority is given to means for constantly assessing and analyzing the current operations of an agency; and these devices serve as important sources of information for the social welfare administrator when he engages in his decision-making activities.

A major goal of social welfare administration is the enhancement of social functioning. More specifically, in regard to the goal of distribution of resources, this model encompasses the

---

Social Welfare Administration: Today and Tomorrow," Council on Social Work Education Annual Program Meeting, 1969 (mimeographed), pp. 4–5. For an interesting "intermediate" model outside social work, see Daniel J. Levinson and Gerald L. Klerman, "The Clinician-Executive," *Psychiatry,* XXX (1967), 3–15.

[14] A NASW committee report outlines some of the behavioral and social science knowledge relevant to social work administration, without reference to the methods issues which have been raised in the past. See *Social Work Administration* (New York: National Association of Social Workers, 1968).

[15] See Katz and Kahn, *op. cit.,* pp. 259–99.

major monitoring and implementing positions in the field of social welfare. Social workers who administer the social welfare goods and services of our society from this perspective are the key group in the profession's attainment of this goal.

SOCIAL ADMINISTRATION

Social administration, although not widely known in American social work, represents a model which has been in existence in Western Europe for several decades.[16] In terms of the continuum here, social administration moves further away from American social work's emphasis on residual functions and the concomitant stress on a model of individual achievement-failure.[17] Social administration moves toward the opinion that knowledge and skills of the profession are interrelated not only with the social sciences but also with the values, priorities, and resources of the larger social institutions. Thus, social administration focuses on the policies, planning, and administration of social welfare goods and services in relation to the political, social, and economic institutions and to the determinants of the distribution of national resources to social welfare needs.

The related term "national development" refers to the broad social and economic resources, and to the establishment of priorities which crucially determine the goals and functions of the social work profession in a given society.[18] In this context, social

[16] See Barbara N. Rodgers, John Greve, and John S. Morgan, *Comparative Social Administration* (New York: Atherton Press, 1968); David Vernon Donnison and Valerie Chapman, *Social Policy and Administration* (London: George Allen & Unwin, Ltd., 1965); Kathleen M. Slack, *Social Administration and the Citizen* (London: Michael Josephs, 1966). For the impact of cybernetics on policy and administration in American social welfare, see Allen Shick, "The Cybernetic State," *Trans-action*, LXX, No. 4 (1970), 15–26.

[17] These features of American social work are described in David M. Austin, "Social Work's Relation to National Development in Developing Nations," *Social Work*, XV, No. 1 (1970), 97–106.

[18] From this perspective, "Social work will champion a planned and comprehensive overhaul of moribund institutions while searching constantly for substitute structures for those which are unjust or unworkable. Emphasis on the macro and intermediate levels of professional intervention will, of necessity, entail a corresponding turning away from such approaches of social work that are geared primarily to enhancing individual adjustment." S. K. Khinduka, "Social Work and the Third World" (1970; mimeographed), p. 20.

administration is directly linked to the social work profession, but from the broader vantage point of social welfare and from the perspective of other social and economic institutional influences on national social welfare development. Compared with the other two models, this approach may be seen as less in the mainstream of American social work. At the same time, it provides a comparative analysis which may indicate new directions and alternatives for the profession, especially as American national priorities and social welfare planning change the distribution of social welfare resources. And we have a questionable illustration of such change in the family assistance program now before Congress.

The major assumptions stem from a macro-view of the social work profession as a subsystem of social welfare which, in turn, is a subsystem of the larger social, political, and economic institutions of society.[19] Thus, while social administration does not deny that social work may initiate, from within its own profession, a definition of its boundaries, practices, and resources, this viewpoint does assume that the perimeters of the profession's initiative are constantly bounded and determined by events in the larger system. Social administration, then, assumes a systems approach within which such social work and social welfare issues as autonomy, interventions, clientele, programs, and agencies are constantly being redetermined by the larger societal context.

Interventions generated by social administration derive from this basis. Thus, interventions are carried out less in terms of isolated administrative decisions than in terms of decisions related to other parts of the system, with special emphasis on a highly differentiated use of manpower resources. In some respects, the social administrator may be regarded as a catalyst upon other individuals and groups in the system, so that they can intervene with alternatives and resources not previously considered. The interventions of the social administrator are constantly determined by the needs, especially the unmet needs, of client-consumer groups of the social welfare agency. His interventions might be

[19] This systems view is illustrated in W. J. M. MacKenzie, *Politics and Social Science* (Baltimore: Penguin Books, 1967). Shick (*op. cit.*, p. 23) predicts that the major analytic constructs for the policy sciences will be "systems and communication nets."

described as those of a middleman between the upper reaches of policy-making and the firsthand implementation of policy.

Goals for social administration include those of the other two models. On the continuum proposed here, this model distinctly concerns itself with the creation of new societal resources for distribution. Social administration, in contrast with the other two models, focuses upon the creation of new social welfare goods and services, upon an institutional function of social welfare.[20]

Social administration, then, is concerned with the redistribution of priorities and resources in the social welfare field. It is concerned with new delivery systems, with the extension of existing social welfare goods and services, and with the creation of new goods and services. Importantly, it claims a legitimate role in the establishment and monitoring of social welfare indicators as a rational base for the redistribution and creation of these goods and services.[21]

To recapitulate, these three models of administration generate differing assumptions, goals, and interventions in regard to social work practice, the profession, and the relationships of these factors to the larger society. At the same time that these models provide an important comparative analysis of administration in social work, they may not reveal some commonalities that cut across the three models. Some of the social work literature on advocacy and social action suggests a range of strategies that may be employed by all social workers, including those in administrative positions.[22] Thus, the conceptualization of the social worker as an administrative activist borrows heavily from some of our advocacy and social action literature, and it suggests some general strategies that may be applicable to all the models on the continuum.

[20] Wilensky and Lebeaux, *op. cit.*
[21] For a description of the importance of these functions, see U.S. Department of Health, Education, and Welfare, *Toward a Social Report* (Washington, D.C.: U.S. Government Printing Office, 1969). For a critique of this report see Michael Springer, "Social Indicators, Reports, and Accounts: toward the Management of Society," *Annals*, Vol. 388 (1970), 1–13.
[22] For a description of some of the new roles and strategies, see Gerald M. Shattuck and John M. Martin, "New Professional Work Roles and Their Integration into a Social Agency Structure," *Social Work*, XIV, No. 3 (1969), 13–20.

ADMINISTRATIVE ACTIVIST

The term "activist" has been used to indicate direct action in both leftist and rightist political matters.[23] Here the term "administrative activist" is used not to imply a specific political ideology but rather to indicate direct administrative action, initiative, and leadership by social work executives.[24] Thus, this perspective counters the stereotyped view of the administrator as a passive pawn of the status quo.

In a general context, an activist orientation tends to be associated with conflict strategies and interventions and with an emphasis on system change. By contrast, consensus strategies tend to be associated with a more conservative orientation and with emphasis upon maintenance of the system. The limited research and literature regarding executives with the master's degree in social work (MSW) suggests that they are in the latter category and that they employ consensus-type strategies and emphasize maintenance of the social welfare administrative system.[25] A recent survey suggests that this is only partially correct. Initial analysis of data collected from a small sample of social work executives finds that they are much more activist-oriented than our literature has so far indicated.

The survey reported here borrows from Epstein's continuum of consensus and conflict type strategies in social work.[26] Through a partial replication of Epstein's study, data were collected from

[23] Seymour Lipset, "Students and Politics in Comparative Perspective," *Daedalus*, XCVII, No. 1 (1968), 1–20.

[24] The term "administrative activism" has been applied to Daniel Moynihan's writings and criticized on the grounds that it "underestimates the persistence of old-fashioned power relationships and conflicts." Michael Harrington, "The New Elite," book review, *Commentary*, XLIX, No 2 (1970), 84. Rothman, responding to some social work objections to activism, states: "An activist, social-change orientation is seen as compatible with democratic process and *not* contrary to the achievement of functional capacity goals." Jack Rothman, "An Analysis of Goals and Roles in Community Organization Practice," *Social Work*, IX, No. 2 (1964), 30.

[25] For example, see W. Joseph Heffernan, Jr., "Political Activity and Social Work Executives," *Social Work*, IX, No. 2 (1964), 18–23; Paul Weinberger, "Executive Inertia and the Absence of Program Modification," in Weinberger, *Perspectives on Social Welfare* (New York: MacMillan, 1969), pp. 387–94.

[26] Irwin Epstein, "Social Workers and Social Action: Attitudes toward Social Action Strategies," *Social Work*, XV, No. 2 (1968), 101–8. Students at the George

Social Work to Social Administration

eighteen executives in the St. Louis area (median age fifty-two years) and from seventy-one social workers who graduated from the George Warren Brown School of Social Work in 1968 and 1969 (median age twenty-nine years). Popular opinion in social work holds that recent social work graduates are more activist-oriented than social work executives, but the survey findings suggest that such a generalization requires important qualifications. While conflict strategies are approved slightly more by the recent graduates than by the executives with the MSW degree, the same strategies are actually used by these executives more frequently than by recent graduates. Thus, on these dimensions, the differences between our executives and recent graduates do not appear to be significant.

Additional interview data from other social work executives suggest that they are, in fact, employing conflict strategies within their own agencies and among their own staff. Basic changes in the system are not necessarily the goals, but, more likely, better service delivery within the system. Thus, some executives may employ conflict strategies to counter staff resistances to change, to increase service productivity, and to create administrative structures which will lead to more effective services delivery.[27]

These conflict strategies are illustrated by an executive of a large staff of social workers in a psychiatric hospital. He has developed his own typology of strategies which include: (1) stimulating change among staff by introducing his own ideas and personal persuasion in staff meetings, conferences, etc.; (2) exposing staff to new ways for delivering social work services by assigning them tasks to explore or developing new delivery systems within or outside the hospital; (3) making explicit use of his own clinical skills in encounter groups with staff, encourag-

---

Warren Brown School of Social Work, in *Social Work 585*, collected and tabulated these data in the fall of 1969.

[27] These statements are drawn from students' written summaries of their tutorials with executives in the St. Louis area. These executives may be similar to those "whose referent is the professional staff of his agency as much as his board, the administrator for whom professional reputation may provide the basis for present or future success, [and who] will not totally ignore the norms of the field in favor of powerful community forces." George A. Brager, "Institutional Change: Perimeters of the Possible," *Social Work*, XII, No. 1 (1967), 65.

ing group discussion of interpersonal conflicts and tensions in work relationships, with the goal that the staff will engage in new treatment modalities and new organizational arrangements for services.[28] This same executive is developing agency structures which foster collegial rather than traditional hierarchical relations among staff. Similar explorations are under way in a number of social agencies.[29]

The administrative activist, then, performs important functions which may cut across all three models of administration. These functions apply regardless of the method employed by the social worker as an administrator. Thus, the administrative activist represents important interventions toward achieving better distribution and use of social welfare programs and services. Yet, in themselves, these strategies do not lead to a focus on the goal of, and the interventions for achieving, new and desperately needed social welfare resources. For these, we must move beyond the administrative activist.

TOWARD NEW SOCIAL WELFARE RESOURCES

An essential step if social work is to deal substantively with the third major goal of social work is to assign some priority and support to the education for, and practice of, the social administration model. Leadership in the NASW has resulted in statements that favor some sort of guaranteed income, document the need for a family allowance system, explicate the arguments for resident control of neighborhood facilities and for effective, grass-roots political participation. Yet the rhetoric of our professional association does not match the reality.

Social workers have had minimal influence because we have had minimal knowledge. We have had minimal knowledge because only a small portion of our educational and practice resources has been deployed to anything more than a residual model of social work knowledge and practice; and this model has dominated our practice as administrators. In our preoccupation

---

[28] Excerpted from paper by William Hunt, George Warren Brown School of Social Work, January, 1970.

[29] See Joseph H. Kahle, "Structuring and Administering a Modern Voluntary Agency, *Social Work*, XIV, No. 1 (1969), 21–28.

with narrower professional concerns, too many of us have defaulted on knowledge leadership which might lead toward the beginning of some institutional functions in American social welfare.

This is not to deny the value of residual social welfare services and programs. Nor is it to suggest that social work's attention to a social administration model will provide a panacea. Yet it will be a beginning by allocating some of our own resources to counterbalance the forces in our society which make it possible for American social welfare still to be characterized by nineteenth-century laissez-faire economics and Social Darwinism. Too much of social work practice can still be subsumed under these characteristics.

We must move, then, beyond only clinical or managerial or activist approaches in social work to a model of social administration which will meet the urban-racial realities of the twentieth-century United States. It must address itself to the diverse interests of our peoples, affirming a nonpathological view of social and personal conflict.[30] It will require that we be less concerned with the autonomy and protection of the social work profession and agencies than with a firm integration of both our values and the facts regarding the disadvantaged and high-risk people who continue to suffer from the benign neglect that results from our current national priorities and our social welfare policies. It will require that we venture beyond the province of our profession to the knowledge and activities in other disciplines and in other arenas of power that can influence the field of social welfare.

[30] For the conceptualization of conflict as a normal social process, see Mary Parker Follett, *Creative Experience* (London: Longmans, Green, and Co., 1924).

Alleviating Tensions in an Ethnic Neighborhood

GLENN W. OLSON

At this time of constant reference to revolution, it is imperative that we develop new approaches to the people who have not "made it" from our ethnic subcultures. There can be little doubt that traditional approaches by the social welfare institutions have failed miserably with the approximately 40 million families in these substructures who are becoming increasingly prone to violence and reactionary movements. It is time that we ask ourselves some key questions: What approaches can alter the violent behavior of working-class people? Can social welfare professionals effectively confront and reduce the alarming rate of polarization in our society? Are there not elements in the black rejection of, and the white backlash reaction to, social welfare which should cause us to rethink our entire traditional approach to problems of the disadvantaged? Why have we not had the same sympathy and empathy for the white ethnics which we have had for other minorities?

During the last two and a half years, through the use of what might be called "sensible politics," Alta House has been building new programs in the Mayfield-Murray Hill section of Cleveland (Little Italy) by careful planning, confrontation, mediation, negotiation, and development of new resources in order to reduce tensions among ethnic groups in an area ideally suited to such efforts.

For several years many leaders in the social welfare field, including the National Federation of Settlements and Neighborhood Centers, have advocated the greater emphasis on community development and neighborhood control that we have achieved with some measure of success. Our first theoretical base, was the comprehensive planning, both physical and social, called for in model cities programs, but financed by private funds. We believe that social and physical problems and their potential solutions are intricately related, that there is no simple cause-and-effect relationship, that there are many problems and many possible solutions without necessarily a direct relationship between any single problem and its solution or solutions.

The second major theoretical base has been conflict theory,[1] the idea that conflict is necessary for change and that an effective change agent capitalizes on conflict to produce desirable changes. In other words, he uses "sensible politics" in a nonpartisan sense.

ETHNIC GROUPS DEFINED

Andrew M. Greeley says:

The ethnic group is a combination of European cultural background, American culturation experience (different for different groups) and political, social, and economic common interests. Not merely do origins produce cultural differences; but different experiences in America reinforce the old difference and create new ones.[2]

Other authorities have proposed a simpler, broader definition; an ethnic group can be considered to be any group in America which shares a common past, present, and anticipated future. This more comprehensive definition makes it possible to consider that membership in groups, such as the social welfare profession, is a functional substitute for an ethnic group identification. Whatever definition we choose, there is no doubt that ethnicity and its substitutes are an important dynamic in our society and that many of us by choosing to ignore it have overlooked a major element which could lead to better understanding of, and new ideas for dealing with, the pressing social problems of America.

One aspect of ethnicity is that there is a basic psychological norm which people ascribe to those whom they consider to be

[1] For further elaborations on the use of conflict theory see Simon Slavin, "Concepts of Social Conflict: Use in Social Work Curriculum," *Journal of Education for Social Work*, V, No. 1 (1969), 47–60.
[2] Andrew M. Greeley, *Why Can't They Be like Us?* (New York: Institute of Human Relations Press, the American Jewish Committee, 1969), pp. 10–11.

of a common origin: the whole idea that "we" are against "them." Ethnicity can become a problem when the ethnic group has the potential for power, when it is well-organized, or when it becomes conscious that it is surrounded by other powerful ethnic groups.

When we begin to understand ethnicity we see, too, that all ethnic groups pass through a similar process of assimilation even though it differs somewhat with each group. Mr. Greeley describes its phases as: (1) cultural shock; (2) organization and emerging self-consciousness; (3) assimilation of the elite; (4) militancy; (5) self-hatred and antimilitancy; and (6) emerging adjustment.[3]

Not all groups go through this process at the same rate as have white Protestant Americans. Some groups, particularly the lower-class whites and blacks, are beginning to believe that the "melting pot" was never really intended to include them because the melting pot was for those people who could be assimilated in a WASP society, and thus some of them have become fixed at a low level of assimilation. Furthermore, if an ethnic group feels that it is under attack, it regresses to an earlier level of assimilation.

Competition is also an important factor. A certain amount of conflict between ethnic groups can lead to progressive changes and adjustments so long as they agree on how to handle their conflicts through means such as political negotiations. But when there are no agreed-upon rules of the game, conflicts frequently break out into violence. Competition occurs throughout the entire range of human affairs, particularly in politics, religion, housing, education, trade unions, business, rackets, and over who is going to get the biggest share of the limited power available.

Economic competition and the mass media add to conflicts. Most lower-class ethnic people work hard at menial, low-paying jobs which are rapidly going out of existence because of automation. Since their wages have not kept up with rising costs of living and they bear a heavy burden of taxation because their taxes have increased at a higher rate than that of suburban residents as

[3] *Ibid.*, pp. 31–37.

tax bases both personal and industrial have diminished in our cities. Most of them have serious financial problems. In addition, they are the defenders of our country since they constitute the majority of our armed services and our police forces.

At the same time, most of these Americans have very little direct contact with their stable working-class black counterparts. Their concept of Negroes is formed from watching television, which capitalizes on "newsworthy" events and produces an image of blacks who create riots and are constantly involved in other violent acts or participating in demonstrations for what white lower-class people consider unreasonable demands.[4] Correspondingly, the mass media also magnify the importance of violence which occurs in ethnic white areas.

Sex is an area of potential conflict which can be very important. Eldridge Cleaver in *Soul on Ice*[5] and Calvin Hernton in *Sex and Racism in America*[6] discuss underlying sexual aspects of conflicts between white ethnic groups and black groups. Both indicate that white people in the United States have perceived black men as intellectually inferior with superior sexual and other physical powers. This assumption can easily lead to violence because it can cause jealousy on the part of white men, who then feel an urgent need to protect their women from the supposedly superior sexual powers of black men. This is of particular significance in Italian communities, for instance, where the admired male image is one of a strong and sexually powerful figure.

LITTLE ITALY

Little Italy is ideally suited for research to gain insights about new approaches to white ethnic groups. A small, geographically isolated area, it has been considered to be the most "hard right" neighborhood in a city known for its large concentrations of ethnic groups. In recent years, Cleveland has had a tremendous

[4] Richard J. Krickus, "40 Million Ethnics Rate More than Bromides," *Washington Post*, August 31, 1969.
[5] Eldridge Cleaver, *Soul on Ice* (New York: Dell Publishing Co., 1968).
[6] Calvin C. Hernton, *Sex and Racism in America* (New York: Grove Press, Inc., 1965). For an excellent bibliography on white ethnics see *White Ethnic America* (New York: American Jewish Committee, 1969).

loss of middle-income whites who have "made it" and a concomitant increase in its black population, leaving it with a majority of both whites and blacks who simply have not "made it."

Little Italy is an old, declining Italian neighborhood which has failed to adjust to the fact that it is no longer a port of entry for Italians in a city which is no longer predominantly a white city. Strong family ties of second- and third-generation Italians, and formidable physical boundaries, fostered the illusion that this was still an intact ethnic community. But the mass exodus of white people from the east side of Cleveland and the corresponding increase in the black population had made Little Italy a small ethnic island unattuned to its surroundings. The expansion of the Case Western Reserve University complex which had taken a large portion of the neighborhood, the decrease in political power of ethnics in Cleveland, along with the election and reelection of Mayor Carl B. Stokes, the recent immigration of approximately a thousand Appalachian whites into the area, and the increased loss of control over their own youngsters, created a state of disequilibrium.

As a result of racial changes in bordering communities, one of the most pressing problems was the high proportion of high school dropouts (nearly three times the city average), which resulted from the local youths' unwillingness to attend predominantly black, educationally inadequate schools, such as John Hay High School. The failure of neighborhood institutions to adapt to the situation, and the inadequacies of Cleveland's city services, especially the Police Department, had further eroded the area and created a sense of hopelessness. As a result, the population has declined since the 1920s from nearly 10,000 people, over 95 percent of whom were Italian, to fewer than 4,000 people, less than 66 percent of whom are of Italian descent.

Little Italy was plagued, too, by a multitude of physical problems, including traffic congestion, lack of open space, insufficient parking space, substandard housing, and the failure of a large number of small family businesses in recent years. Nevertheless, the neighborhood had a chance of surviving and prospering in the future if it modified its violent behavior, because its population was still quite stable and it has a very good location near a large cultural complex.

Little Italy was known as a bastille of the "hard right" in Cleveland, the scene of several attacks on blacks in recent years. What accounted for this behavior? The people in Little Italy are part of 40 million white families in the United States with family incomes ranging from $5,000 to $10,000 who consider themselves the "forgotten Americans" because they belong neither to the poor black population which, they believe, receives special treatment, nor to America's affluent middle and upper classes.

Furthermore, Italians were one of the last immigrant groups to achieve a measure of equality in the United States. Since legitimate opportunities were not generally available to them until the late 1930s, many achieved success illegally by violence and through organized crime. Others achieved upward mobility through political organizations when more "respectable" channels were closed to them.

The dropouts of the neighborhood's street-corner society reacted to the threat of change as though no change had occurred in the status of Italians since the 1930s. The breakdown of the community's Italian culture represents to them a return to minority status. (As a matter of fact, they *are* once again in a minority status, since they are surrounded by blacks in the eastern part of Cleveland and must attend predominantly black public high schools.) Furthermore, as the upwardly mobile Italians leave, those who have failed to "make it," are experiencing a downward mobility and have moved into the militancy phase of assimilation. This downward mobility, in turn, breaks down the traditional family relationships, resulting in almost total lack of parental and other adult control of these young men, thereby increasing their intolerance of other minorities and their propensity toward violence. The high school dropouts became the hard-core "protectors" of a dying neighborhood, motivated by the desire to defend their own "turf," and acting in typical lower-class style by perpetuating violent attacks on outsiders—behavior very similar to that seen in black areas under great pressure.

ALTA HOUSE

Alta House is a seventy-one-year-old settlement house whose program grew out of the nineteenth-century reform movement led by upper-middle-income board and staff members who wanted to help disadvantaged immigrants in Little Italy learn middle-class ways in order that they might become assimilated in the Greater Cleveland area. Its primary activity was character-building programs which could counteract the bad influences of the environment. These functions were useful years ago when a large proportion of the community residents were upwardly mobile; they were not relevant to the factors which contribute to racial tensions, as was evident from the decreasing membership and the total failure of the organization to reach the potentially violent young men of the neighborhood.

Recognizing the failure of traditional casework and group work approaches geared to problem management, Alta House initiated a self-help community development project to deal with the real causes of neighborhood problems. One of the major strategies called for changing antisocial behavior by modifying the local opportunity structure through economic development techniques. Basically, this strategy involved assisting the second-generation leaders in becoming successful neighborhood businessmen whose establishments would attract many outside people as customers; leaders of the community would then have a vested interest in protecting the outsiders from violent acts by resident youths. This private project began by organizing a powerful *ad hoc* power structure through a neighborhood development corporation which would conduct a model cities type of social and physical planning effort. Using physical planning as a wedge to get at the social problems of the neighborhood, we hoped to modify the leaders' attitudes toward outsiders.

Another major strategy was that of developing a new social control mechanism to supplant the old system of protection by violence. Block clubs were organized on each street to cope with the problems on that street, and a neighborhood-wide association

Tensions in an Ethnic Neighborhood

of block clubs was set up to cope with problems that individual clubs could not handle.

Research had documented the fact that nearly all the delinquents came from marginal-income families. Consequently, a series of guided mobility programs was instituted to help these people achieve stable lower-class status. These programs, operated by the settlement, consist of preschool training, budget counseling, job training and placement, a street academy for high school dropouts, and other group services designed to help youths remain in school.

Many of the traditional recreational and informal educational functions of the settlement house were later transferred to the city Board of Education's Recreation Department in order to permit the settlement house to become more problem-focused.

Throughout the process we have used conflict theory to bring about change through the use of nonpartisan politics as conflicts arose.

The *ad hoc* power structure was established quite successfully with a combination of neighborhood people who were apparent leaders, a few talented and politically astute agency board members, and a small nucleus of advocate social and physical planners. The development corporation drew up a sophisticated plan on a relatively low-cost budget. When the initial plan was submitted in a slide film presentation and discussed block by block, it received an overwhelming endorsement, probably because most people recognized that the neighborhood would not survive without some improvements and others thought that the plan would help build higher the walls which already isolated Little Italy. However, we failed to make any physical improvements which people could identify with the corporation, and a large segment of the community leadership felt left out.

Although the feeling of being left out was not evident at that time, it certainly became clear when the corporation issued its final report, which called for a $25 million plan for redeveloping the neighborhood. This document stated clearly that violent attacks on innocent outsiders must stop if the neighborhood was to survive. The purpose of this was to bring the issue of the attacks out into the open in order to establish new "rules" for resolving conflicts with bordering communities. That set off a series of reactions by the leaders of another segment of the area's power structure. For the first time the real leaders of the youths on the street corners came out of obscurity and openly challenged the redevelopment plan. They staged shout-ins, picketed, put up hostile signs damning the development corporation, and burned the director of Alta House in effigy; some youths even walked around with pistols and threatened to shoot him. Needless to say, there was enough conflict to produce change; in fact, many of us were concerned that the conflict might have gone beyond a point where it could be used to produce constructive change.

Therefore, our strategy was to reduce the conflict by giving the newly emerged leaders a chance to ventilate their feelings through their shout-ins and to try to co-opt the more responsible leaders by electing them to the settlement house board of trustees and encouraging them to compete with the traditional, ineffective neighborhood leaders for membership on the board of directors of the neighborhood citizens organization.

This strategy has worked well to date; it really has helped the out-group of neighborhood leaders become involved in bringing about the community control which many of us have been advocating for years. As the new leaders became involved, the *ad hoc* power structure of the development corporation was dropped, and the struggle took on an entirely new dimension. When we succeeded in placing new leaders in power positions, we correspondingly had to give up some power ourselves, including power over our own agency. In other words, "community control" is a mixed blessing and especially so in a racially tense neighborhood.

Now that there is a renewed sense of togetherness and pride and people feel that they can control their neighborhood, we are looking forward to the possibility that this community can work together with other people on common problems. They are already forming a coalition with middle- and upper-income Italians from "outside" in order to produce needed resources for their neighborhood center and housing rehabilitation programs. Moreover, a political coalition with blacks is clearly within the realm of possibility.

An excerpt from the Cleveland *Plain Dealer* about a reception in Little Italy is significant: "Mayor Carl B. Stokes—the same Carl B. Stokes who told a companion during a European tour earlier this year: 'I take you to see the Pope, and you can't take me to Murray Hill'—was welcomed in that part of town last night like a long-lost paisano." [7]

The new leaders have now come around to supporting almost all of the plans of the development corporation, including the control of violence by helping alienated youth who are prone to antisocial behavior and by working toward a better adjustment to society through a street academy, job development, and other supportive programs. Furthermore, the self-help aspects of the physical improvement in the area have succeeded unusually well; over 20 percent of the homes are already rehabilitated. In addition, the residents have a renewed interest in their Italian heritage and identification with their neighborhood which may be seen as movement toward the self-hatred and antimilitancy phase of assimilation. Essentially, we have achieved a new state of equilibrium with redefined rules of the game and shifted from a violent approach for solving conflicts to a political one which eventually may lead to healthy collaboration with other ethnic groups in Cleveland.

The new dimensions of conflict have placed a great deal of pressure on the staff of Alta House, for neighborhood people are constantly demanding changes. Secondly, it forces the director to become a politician who can negotiate their demands and interests with old board members, with funding sources such as the community council and United Appeal, with other vital interests in the greater community, and with many people who lean toward the opposite extreme in their political and social views. Thus, the director and his staff are constantly involved in risk in this political arena.

Social workers must recognize that there are both positive and

[7] Cleveland *Plain Dealer,* May 21, 1970.

negative aspects in our own identification with the social welfare field. We have not recognized our own prejudice toward lower-class ethnic people. This became evident to me when my social work friends implied that I was helping the enemy by aiding "those people." Furthermore, those who criticized me the most had very little insight into the real nature of neighborhoods such as this, which they readily called "white racist," thinking that that had solved the problem. This attitude only made them feel superior to these disadvantaged people and, in fact, contributed to the problems. If they had looked objectively at the real cause of tension in our inner cities they would have found that it is related to the fact that the large numbers of middle- and upper-income people who have left our inner cities are draining it of its wealth, spending most of their own money in the suburbs. The affluent have drawn a noose around our inner cities which is getting tighter each day as suburbanites, professional social workers included, are becoming even more affluent.

Secondly, we have not honestly been willing to admit that there has been something paternalistic and manipulative about our traditional approaches. This, it seems, has been brought out by the recent rejection of social workers by blacks and increasing reaction against them by lower-income whites. Although we have advocated community control and self-determination, we have really wanted to have our cake and eat it as well. We wanted those ideals, but with the one condition that we could continue to control people. Finally, do we not add to the polarization between lower-income whites and blacks by accusing lower-class ethnic whites of being "racists" because we just are not willing to face the real issue that the problems of lower-income whites are almost identical with those of lower-income blacks? Unless our society helps both with massive redistributions of funds, so that those people who need a good education, good housing, employment, and city services receive their fair share, the individual's freedom cannot survive, and we will all see a police state developing in our country to protect our own affluent turf.

Beyond Advocacy: a New Model for Community Organization

PAUL A. KURZMAN and
JEFFREY R. SOLOMON

THE ROLE OF COMMUNITY ORGANIZATION in social work is undergoing questioning and revision. The profession, seeking legitimization, insists that all its methods maintain a scientific form designed to conquer the variables which are omnipresent in human relationships. Community organization practitioners, who were rather recently accepted in the professional ranks, therefore attempt to devise techniques to make community organization a legitimate social work function. Consequently, community organization, like other social work methods, becomes more concerned with professional techniques and jargon than with the basic questions concerning effective practice.

Here we shall deal with the dilemma of trying to maintain professionalism and still be creative and productive at the same time. We seek no one methodological approach to the problems of the community. Rather, we offer a means by which communities may be organized, seeking to utilize the most positive aspects of traditional social work as well as newer approaches to community organization method and practice. Implicit in this goal is the recognition that, similar to social movements in contemporary America, the professions too are gliding through a phase of "doing your own thing," leaving in question the absoluteness of any community organization dogma. Social work, therefore, may now be ready to test out doctrine in day-to-day practice. This approach, analogous to *consensus fidelum* in the Church, permits codification of the practice by the institution after the fact. For example, Vatican II engaged in various forms of *consensus fidelum* in regard to its positions, questioning much of the past history. This was done in recognition of change within both religious institutions and secular society.

THE ADVOCACY DILEMMA

Recent thinking within social work, including community organization, provides what seems to be an irreconcilable theoretical framework. On the one hand, the traditional social worker espouses client self-determination as leading to greater client independence. On the other hand, a leading school of thought in community organization calls for advocacy practice by the professional community organizer.[1] Charles Grosser, for example, makes the analogy between the social work advocate and the legal advocate, pointing out the professional ramifications of each one's role. One essential difference (requiring careful consideration if one is to utilize the advocate's role in social work) is the constraints of the social agency. The profession of law traditionally is practiced on the basis of the independence of each attorney in acting on behalf of his clients. The exercise of any type of restraint on an attorney's advocacy results in unconscionable, and perhaps unethical, practice. This is not necessarily the case in social work. Executives of agencies must be prepared for backlash when their staffs engage in advocacy. This backlash may come from the board of directors, professional colleagues, the community, or from sources of funding. How does the executive act when these pressures are upon him? Are there not additional constraints placed on an advocate by agency policies? Is this not a perversion of the legal principle of advocacy independence?

Mayer Zald points out the various factors that come into play in the daily operation of the community organization agency. He sees the practitioner not as a free agent, but rather as limited by the goals and politics of the agency.[2] This premise may be further expanded to include the agency executive, who sees himself as limited by the goals and politics of the agency board. George Brager points out:

[1] Charles F. Grosser, "Community Development Programs Serving the Urban Poor," *Social Work*, X, No. 3 (1965), 15–21.

[2] Mayer N. Zald, "Organizations as Politics: an Analysis of Community Organization Agencies," *Social Work*, XI, No. 4 (1966), 56–65.

Social welfare organizations are socially dependent. Since they are not financially self-supporting, they must accommodate to relevant publics. A relationship inevitably exists between an organization's fund-raising base and its willingness to press for institutional change. The class location and value commitments of the major donors are, of course, primary in this regard. Organizational decision-making is thus affected by powerful community forces to which institutional change may be unsettling.[3]

Brager's contentions are relevant to the constraints placed upon the advocate—constraints generally not permitted to be placed upon the law advocate (the basis of the social work model). Whether funding stems from the private or the public sector, prohibitions are placed on an agency which filter down to the practitioner.

While it might be ideal to have community organizers work in private practice, like attorneys, in order to avoid some of these constraints, the economics of the practitioner-client relationship does not make such an alternative feasible at this point. A means of moving toward this direction, however, would be the institution of "Sociocare," which would entitle social work practitioners to the same remuneration received by physicians under Medicare.[4] In such a system, the social worker would be bound by the client's selection of agency and worker and by the ethics of the profession rather than by the requirements of a social agency. It is a possible professional alternative to agency practice. Now is the time, perhaps, for the social work profession to recognize the advantages of private practice in community organization.

THE DEPENDENCY DILEMMA

It seems to this writer that where true advocacy exists, client self-determination is difficult to implement, because the advocate generally determines the best course of action to achieve the client's end. Advocate determination rather than client determination tends to establish a client dependency upon the practitioner which is counter to the tradition and goals of social work.

[3] George A. Brager, "Institutional Change: Perimeters of the Possible," *Social Work*, XII, No. 1 (1967), 61.
[4] For further discussion, see Irving Piliavin, "Restructuring the Provision of Social Services," *Social Work*, XIII, No. 1 (1968), 34–41.

Further, it seems wasteful to establish a core of professionally trained advocates, when legal training is geared to provide the most effective confrontation expert. While the social work advocate has become a quasi-legal spokesman for the poor, he is functioning as such with only a few of the tools needed to meet his ends and the goals of the client. He is not a member of the bar, does not have the professional recognition accorded to an attorney, is unable to advocate in judicial settings, and has never received the exposure to legal procedures and rhetoric that is an integral part of a lawyer's training. It is essential, therefore, that we find the means of altering the traditional advocate role to bring advocacy closer to the ethic of social work.

A PROPOSED MODEL

In the proposed model, three distinct worker roles are envisioned. They follow the historical development of a group, and the worker's transition from one role to the next is a key factor in his effectiveness as a practitioner and in his success in building a self-reliant community organization.

It might be noted that while it is advantageous to have the same worker play all three roles (moving appropriately from one role to the next), the Mississippi experience of the Michael Schwerner Memorial Fund has indicated that different workers may practice at each of these junctures. The roles outlined below are those of organizer-advocate, organizer-educator, and organizer-technical assistant.

PHASE I: WORKER AS ORGANIZER-ADVOCATE

The initial phase of the method entails utilization of the traditional advocate role as defined, for example, by Grosser. Here, the organizer takes on the function of an activist attorney, marshaling resources and arguing the case with, and on behalf of, his clients.

This role assumes that: (1) the worker can better achieve early victories than the client group; (2) the worker will maintain a lawyer-client relationship, compromising only when it is in the interest of the clients; and (3) fears of the institutions will begin to diminish as clients survive confrontation with the system, and —with their advocate's planful assistance—begin to win both real and symbolic victories.

This last point is extremely significant in organizing poor people, especially blacks in the Deep South. Paul Kurzman speaks of a *"Negeya* bond" which may exist between blacks and whites, natives and settlers, clients pushing for change and representatives of the target institutions.[5] The client feels that it is the will of God that permits the system to control so much of his life, and therefore his acceptance of the existing order must methodically be broken down. The nature of involvement during Phase I permits the organizer-advocate to prove that change is indeed possible, and that no tragic outcome will stem from confrontation of the system. The client who has been brought up bound by this *Negeya* bond may begin to question its validity when he sees that he and the advocate are not struck down when they confront the institutions, and that change, not status quo, may be the outcome.

One notion that runs through all phases of the model is the importance of the joint confrontation, with the client observing and participating in every negotiation and confrontation. While it is important for attorneys to approach the bench, to negotiate outside the courtroom, and to meet privately in judges' chambers, in social work practice it is of paramount significance that the client group be an integral part (at least as observers) of every contact with the opposition.

PHASE II: WORKER AS ORGANIZER-EDUCATOR

This role marks the transition from advocacy and dependence to the beginning of a community development model. The worker now focuses on transmission of knowledge and development of leadership within the client group. The group should have reached the transition between Kurzman's Stage 1 and Stage 2 in terms of their reactions to the *Negeya* bond.[6] The worker recognizes that he must begin to withdraw from the participation-

[5] Paul A. Kurzman, "The Native-Settler Concept: Implications for Community Organization," *Social Work*, XIV, No. 3 (1969), 58–64.
[6] *Ibid.*, p. 62.

advocacy role, and instead must enable indigenous leadership to become equipped with the skills which have proved effective in achieving group goals.

Certain specific skills must be transferred and certain tasks performed in order to gain these desired ends. The most essential of these include:

1. *Observation.* The client leaders must be able to share all confrontation experiences with the organizer. For example, in welfare rights organizing, the worker during Phase I should have a client leader or group member present at all advocacy attempts. Gradually, in Phase II, the advocacy responsibility during any such experience must be given to the client-advocate, with the prior preparation and continuing presence of the professional worker.

2. *Technical training.* The client group must be prepared for confrontation with the system. Workshops and training classes must be held so that the clients become well versed in the technical data required in the given setting. This may include knowledge of welfare laws and administrative codes, educational policy, housing codes, and so forth. In confrontations during Phase II, nothing is more upsetting to target system personnel than facing clients who are better versed in their own policies than themselves.

3. *Role play.* The use of simulation and role play is extremely helpful in this phase of organization. They are useful in sensitizing client groups to the very real tasks that lie ahead. Further, they provide meaningful tests of leadership as well as an indication of just how far the group has progressed in mastering the technical knowledge required for future confrontations. An additional factor relates to the *Negeya* bond. The client, through staged confrontations with a white professional worker, begins to play out his rebellion against the system.[7] As he liberates himself from the *Negeya*, it becomes easier for him first to confront his worker, whom he has identified as an ally and who seems more like a "native" than a "settler," than to confront the system he

---

[7] See Robert W. Friedrichs, "Interpretation of Black Aggression," *Yale Review,* LVII (1968), 358–74.

Beyond Advocacy

has always been told to fear. After achieving relative comfort in these training simulations, confronting the system itself is a logical next step in the organizing sequence.

In traditionally black-white settings, the utilization of a white worker to play the role of a white system agent allows the black client a confrontation with a representative of the repressive society. Such a plan seems much closer to reality in this type of setting than in one where a *Negeya* bond exists for other than racial reasons.

Performance during the organizer-educator phase is perhaps the most crucial in attaining a strong, independent group. The worker is tempted to retain his position of control toward the group, which runs counter to the successful completion of Phase II. The demands upon the adaptational skills of the community organization worker are therefore worth noting.

PHASE III: WORKER AS ORGANIZER-TECHNICAL ASSISTANT

The worker's role in Phase III is such that his presence is rarely seen by the community at large. The group's indigenous leadership is in the forefront, and the organizer assumes various advisory roles which they determine. Transition into Phase III is potentially the most difficult for both worker and client. Both skill and sensitivity are required during this delicate procedure. For in a short period of time, the worker must move (or be moved) out of a position of visible influence and must disengage himself from any residual power he still possesses. In this phase, he begins to serve as a consultant on technical matters, and frequently as an agent for continued leadership development and training within the group.

Here again, the role of the worker is key to successful organizational maintenance and group cohesion. His role is that of a catalyst rather than an actor, yet he must be cognizant of the group process. His leadership must be the good leadership of Lao Tse: "A leader is where the people hardly know he exists, but a good leader, when the work is done, the aim fulfilled . . . they will say, 'we did this ourselves.'"

Illustrations of application of this model may be found in the early history of the Hinds County (Mississippi) welfare rights movement. Beginning in May, 1967, the Michael Schwerner Memorial Fund's Mississippi project engaged in direct advocacy on behalf of welfare recipients as the first phase of a welfare rights organizing effort.

Organizers from the Schwerner Fund's local community development agency, following the same minimum standards accepted by departments of welfare throughout the nation, initiated a massive drive to bring welfare recipients in Hinds County up to the minimum standards mandated by law. The volunteer organizers consciously took on the roles of leader and advocate for the clients.

As the movement progressed into the summer, Schwerner Fund workers began a training program on welfare laws and on techniques appropriate to challenging the system. The internal structure of the movement gradually crystallized, with indigenous leadership taking the major roles as the program developed. Group training, sensitivity sessions, role play, and significant plenary involvement permitted a great number of clients to learn the techniques of organizing. It was at this juncture that the National Welfare Rights Organization held its first convention. Leaders of the Hinds County movement who attended that convention strengthened their skills and group identity in this setting, and Phase II became an actuality.

Due to the limited time that the volunteers spent in Mississippi, Phase III never had an opportunity to become reality. However, the initial steps were undertaken. Volunteers significantly removed themselves from positions of influence within the movement. Their assistance was primarily that of providing the technical know-how on laws, bureaucracy, and system confrontation. In practice, volunteers found that they met with client groups both prior to and after confrontations. Often, a passer-by would note the volunteers standing across the street from the welfare office, while clients, under their own leadership, met with public welfare officials.

The consultant or technical assistant role described in Phase III is perhaps the most significant part of the model. It meets the need of both client and practitioner. The client, who must break from patterns of dependence, is able to direct his own movements and the future of his organization. Even though it is difficult to remove oneself from the center of a movement, the worker too may find a significant role for himself in consultation and technical assistance.

We have explored some of the limitations for social work (as an agency-based profession) in embracing the legal-model of advocacy, and we have attempted to reconcile the ideological gap between advocacy and the social work ethic of client self-determination. Community organization, we are convinced, must go *beyond advocacy,* toward a community development model consistent with the long-range goals of social work practice. The ultimate value of this strategy, however, will await its repeated use in a variety of settings by community organization practitioners who are committed to client self-determination, and to social change.

Ethical and Political Issues in Social Research

CAROL H. WEISS

EVERY RESEARCH INVESTIGATION that involves human subjects raises ethical and political issues. Every researcher faces, if only implicitly or by default, questions about the choice of a topic, questions about the uses of his findings, as well as questions about his relationship and responsibilities to the people he is studying.

As social research grows in scope, visibility, and influence, ethical and political issues assume increasing importance. Today challenges are arising to the activities and even to the basic premises and organization of the applied research system. Researchers themselves, as well as subjects and clients, are becoming aware of the consequences of research decisions for themselves, for nonconformist "subject" groups, and for the society.

THREATS TO THE WELFARE OF PARTICIPANTS

The first disciplines that manifested concern about the "human use of human subjects" were those whose research posed the greatest threat to life, limb, and sanity. Thus, surgery, pharmacology, and, more recently, experimental psychology have been concerned about the rights of research subjects, concentrating on the welfare of the individual participant.

1. *Physical or mental harm.* Medicine and pharmacology have sensitized us to the serious impact that research procedures can have on experimental subjects.[1] If the subject is ill, even incurably ill, the experimental procedure may offer him the first hope

[1] Martin M. Katz, "Ethical Issues in the Use of Human Subjects in Psychopharmacologic Research," *American Psychologist*, XXII (1967), 360–63.

Ethical and Political Issues in Research

available, and there are few ethical problems about offering it. In fact, sometimes the issue is whether the same hope should be denied to other sufferers, and researchers have to justify their control group design in the service of knowledge. On the other hand, when they undertake research on normal subjects, investigators have to be seriously concerned about the possibility of producing deleterious physical changes and harmful psychological effects. A study on the effects of LSD, for example, may create long-lasting harm. Without such study, the potentials of drugs will go unexamined.

The usual approach to studies that involve possible harm to subjects is to obtain "informed consent." The subject is given all available information about the danger he is running, and he voluntarily—with no explicit or implicit pressure—decides whether or not to participate. Special concern about children usually means that a parents' consent is required for participation.

2. *Deception.* A second type of threat to human values lies in the deliberate deception of research subjects. Researchers are not inherently crooked souls, but there are experiments—particularly psychological experiments—where disclosure of research purposes and the possible effects would vitiate the study. If the subject knew that the investigator was examining group leadership processes or obedience to authority, for example, he would not be able to behave naturally. Only through misleading instructions to "naïve subjects" will the experiment work.

Many of these psychological experiments by their very nature are stressful. They purposely subject the participant to pressures beyond those of daily living in order to gauge and analyze his responses. Milgram, for example, in his famous experiments on obedience, instructed subjects to administer electric shocks to victims. He told them that the experiment had to do with the effects of pain on learning. The learner-victim was strapped into a chair in an adjoining room, and each time he gave a wrong answer, the subject was to administer a shock of increasing voltage. The electric shock generator was marked not only with voltage numbers but with such warning messages as, "Extreme Intensity Shock" and "Danger: Severe Shock." The machine, of course, was only a dummy, but as the voltage presumably increased, the victim pounded on the wall and finally fell utterly silent. The results of the experiment showed that the majority of subjects, although they made some verbal objections continued to administer shocks way past the "danger" point; in fact, through the very last key on the shock generator.[2] Participation in an experiment of this kind and realization of what one's behavior has meant can hardly fail to have psychological consequences for the subject.

Psychologists are paying more attention now to briefing and debriefing subjects, telling them enough at the start to screen out unwilling participants and trying to counter harmful aftereffects through explanation and counseling. Partly, it is a matter of the survival of the laboratory experiment; if too much resistance develops, the supply of subjects (particularly among students, who provide most grist to the experimental mill) will dwindle. But even more, it is a matter of the morality of researchers. They do not intend to damage their subjects, but their zeal for knowledge may betray their humanistic impulses. They have to become more aware of the dangers of their work and more adept in avoiding or overcoming them.[3] The morality of doing some kinds of experiments at all is a topic of lively debate.

3. *Invasion of privacy.* A third type of threat involves violation of the individual's privacy. To some degree, almost every social research study violates privacy. Often the respondent is a willing partner in the violation, only too eager to pour out his story into the sympathetic ear of the researcher. On occasion, however, people are reluctant to talk about their earnings or their adoption of a child or their history of physical or mental illness, or to be tested, observed, examined. Yet they may be cowed into participation. Whether it is the status of the interviewer, the sanctity surrounding the concept of research, the reluctance to be impolite to a pleasant worker who is trying to do his job, a feeling of obligation to help researchers seek solutions to social problems, a fear

---

[2] Stanley Milgram, "Behavioral Study of Obedience," *Journal of Abnormal and Social Psychology,* LXVII (1963), 371–78.

[3] Herbert C. Kelman, "Human Use of Human Subjects: the Problem of Deception in Social Psychological Experiments," *Psychological Bulletin,* LXVII (1967), 1–11.

that they will lose some benefits if they refuse to cooperate—whether for these or other reasons, people often go along with studies even when they are disinclined to do so.

Some research uses captive populations. The subjects are prison inmates, soldiers, hospital patients, school children, who have little choice about participation. And at least one "outside" household survey, the United States Census, requires cooperation under penalty of law (although no one has ever been prosecuted for refusing to answer Census questions). If subjects' rights are truly a matter of concern, the right to refuse to cooperate is a basic one.[4] No one has yet seriously proposed that researchers, like policemen, inform all contacts of their right to refuse to talk. Unlike police interrogation, research questions are generally superficial and innocuous, and the threat remote. But in cases where sensitive topics are involved, such as drug use, draft evasion, riot activities, perhaps such notification would not be unreasonable. Certainly the researcher will encourage participation by pointing out all the precautions he is taking to guarantee confidentiality and anonymity and stressing the potential value of his research. But no respondent should feel under threat (even if it is no more serious than the threat of getting lower grades in a sophomore course) for failure to participate in research that he deems not in his best interest.

4. *Threats to confidentiality.* All researchers are aware of the need to protect respondents' anonymity. Names are removed from tests, questionnaires, and interview schedules, and code numbers assigned. Locked files prevent protocols from falling into the hands of unauthorized people. Social anthropologists disguise the names and attributes of individuals in their reports or combine characteristics into composites to forestall identification of individuals. Sociologists release no responses or tabular data which would allow the identification of individuals or small groups. Confidentiality is one of the most sacred and strictly observed of research canons.

[4] Executive Office of the President, Office of Science and Technology, *Privacy and Behavioral Research* (Washington, D.C.: Government Printing Office, 1967); summarized in *American Psychologist,* XXII (1967), 345–49.

Nevertheless, two developments are making clear that, despite all the precautions taken, research data are not invulnerable to penetration. The first is the growth of the idea of a national data system. Such a system would integrate the vast quantities of data on individuals that are currently tucked away in diverse files, and make them available for cross analysis. It would start with data in federal archives but could be expanded to include state and local records and even private records, such as credit ratings, insurance files, and hotel registrations. It could assemble and link up records for each individual on such items as birth, school test scores, driver's license, Selective Service experience, arrests and convictions, tax forms, marriage and divorce, and allow analysts to examine the interrelationships among the data. Such a system has enormous attraction as a resource for researchers interested in understanding the complexities of behavior and social conditions, and as a means of reducing redundancies in data collection and thus lowering its cost. But it requires that data on each individual be identified so that it can be matched with other items about him. The potential availability of the data for nonresearch purposes has disquieting "1984" overtones.

In the past, privacy has been protected by the high cost of assembling data from different sources. Now with computers and an increasingly sophisticated technology for processing and storing data, it is possible to collect and store data equivalent to a 300-page book on every living American on just forty 4800-foot tapes.[5] Few can doubt that, if such a system were in existence, there would be pressures to use the information for what are deemed important social purposes: to decide on employment of applicants for federal jobs; to detect crime and subversion; to grant passports or fellowships, and for similar "worthy" purposes. From there, it is not a long step to political surveillance and police control.

There would not only be formidable temptations to use the data for official control; as the system moved into intercomputer linkages there would be increased opportunities for unauthorized

[5] Jack Sawyer and Howard Schechter, "Computers, Privacy and the National Data Center: the Responsibility of Social Scientists," *American Psychologist*, XXIII (1968), 810–18.

snooping. Specialists can design rigorous safeguards and complicated transformations, but no system is completely immune to code-breaking.

Certainly a national data system offers overwhelming research advantages. But as Westin has said, "privacy is an irreducibly critical element in the operation of individuals, groups, and government in a democratic system with a liberal culture." [6] More thought has to go into safeguards and sanctions. Sawyer and Schechter recommend explicit legal penalities for use of any data on individuals by anyone. The cost of breaking the system must be made financially prohibitive and politically untenable. Furthermore, until we can demonstrate that current data resources are being fully and wisely exploited, I suggest that we give careful second thoughts to the whole concept of integrating individual records and consider alternative and less hazardous schemes for studying complex social phenomena.

Another recent development has highlighted the fragility of our standard guarantees about the confidentiality and anonymity of research data. That is the action taken by police to subpoena newspapermen's notes and records on such subjects as the Black Panthers. It is clear that under law, research interviews and records are equally susceptible to subpoena. Research data are not privileged in the way that communications to lawyers or clergymen are. If the police require information for the prosecution of a case, legal opinion appears to be that the researcher is obligated to produce his material. If he refuses, he is committing a crime.

The likelihood of police use of research data appears remote. For one thing, it is possible only in those cases where a researcher is known to have interviewed a person suspected of illegal activity. More important, police agencies tend to be uninterested in research data; they prefer their own investigation procedures. That no issue has yet arisen is probably due more to this preference for police methods than to any ethical concerns about the violation of research ethics. The possibility for trouble remains.

5. *Cessation of research demonstrations.* In recent years there have been a large number of "demonstration" projects funded

[6] Alan F. Westin, *Privacy and Freedom* (New York: Atheneum, 1967), p. 368.

with the avowed purpose of testing out innovative approaches to social welfare programming. Usually the demonstration is given a finite life span; organizations are created, services are provided, new methods and structures are tried out and evaluated. Once the demonstration period is over, the project is terminated. Even when research shows that the project has had beneficial effects, the funding organization withdraws its funds with the expectation that local agencies will adopt and continue the activities.

Often, of course, the withdrawal of outside funds signals the end of the project. The participants who have come to depend on the project are abandoned. They have served their purpose as "subjects" for the project's evaluation. Neither the researchers nor the program practitioners can do more than try to refer them to other, possibly nonexistent, services.

It is not only the researcher who may have qualms about the plight of project participants. The whole strategy of the research-demonstration as a stimulus to social change may well need reexamination. Experience indicates that it has not been a resounding success in its larger goals of inducing organizations to alter basic modes of operation. Certainly the welfare of abandoned participants deserves consideration as new means are sought to make agencies more relevant and responsive to social needs.

So far, we have considered threats to human values and have raised ethical issues that concern the health, adjustment, privacy, and anonymity of the individual respondent. There are also problems at the level of the collectivity. Research can create risks for groups and subcultures in the society. These kinds of issues move us into the political realm.

Every time we choose a topic for research, we are making a political decision. The manner in which we structure an inquiry, the group we select to study, the questions we decide to raise, are politically relevant decisions.[7] We accept some features of the system as given and others as subject to study and change. Because most of us share the dominant values of the society, we are rarely conscious of the assumptions we make. But at a time when so-

[7] Gideon Sjoberg and Roger Nett, *A Methodology for Social Research* (New York, Evanston, Ill. and London: Harper & Row, 1968), pp. 117–24.

cietal values come under attack, the salience and the political content of research decisions become manifest. Today, for example, research that helps the military establishment is anathema on college campuses, and faculty members are reconsidering their priorities and responsibilities.

6. *The definition of social problems.* One of the threats that research can pose is the definition of social issues in irrelevant or outmoded terms. Thus, researchers can study problems of poverty to discover what is wrong with the poor that prevents them from getting ahead. Or they can do research on what kinds of services poor people need and which of these services are lacking in the community. Even when such conceptual approaches fail to produce solutions, researchers may persist in them rather than devoting attention to fundamental issues about the stratification system of the society, the distribution of power, and the distribution and possible redistribution of income. Perhaps poverty research today should center on the means of insuring that poor people are no longer poor.

In similar vein, researchers can study the effectiveness of educational programs for ghetto youth in terms of whether they succeed or fail (whatever the criteria). Such a definition is useful only for making a decision on whether to continue the programs or abandon them. But this is an inadequate definition of the issue. If we have a commitment to improve education, then our evaluation studies have to go beyond the succeed-or-fail model and tell us how to make the programs better. Evaluations have to inquire into which components of educational programs are more effective than others, which program variations are more successful, which directions are fruitful for further investment. (We may also need more basic research on the processes of learning.)

Anthropologists have become particularly sensitive to the effects of their research in defining and structuring political concepts. At recent professional meetings, they have hotly debated such issues about research in black ghettos as these: Has research functioned as an instrument of imperialism, as a way of learning enough about lower-class black culture to "cool out" the dissidents? Should researchers wait until they are invited into a community by the residents? Should researchers always study the poor and not the government functionaries who run the institutional network and control their lives, much as anthropologists under colonialism studied the aborigines and never the colonial administration?

At a time of conflict and cleavage, the political implications of social research can raise fundamental questions. There are those who now question the motives and value systems of researchers. They accuse researchers of being so preoccupied with their careers, their positions in the university, the government grant system, and the prestige order that they avoid raising uncomfortable issues or "making waves." These critics accuse researchers of using respondents for their own professional gain and avoiding their accountability to the people they subject to study.

Traditionally, people engaged in applied social research have been reformers. We want to do good, not revolutionize society but increase its effectiveness in remedying social ills. It comes as a shock to find that radicals see us as part of the corrupt establishment. But if we persist in studying problems in terms of outmoded models, we are, in fact, helping to perpetuate inadequate definitions of social problems, and we are contributing to inadequate political prescriptions.

7. *Use of research results.* An issue akin to that of defining research problems concerns the uses that are made of research findings and the extent of the researcher's responsibility to the people he studies. Research can be used to advance their social, political, and economic interests as they define them; it can be irrelevant to them; or it can be used to manipulate them for the purposes of others or of social order.

The researcher usually perceives his role as doing the best and most objective research of which he is capable. He reports not only to the body that pays for it but through professional publications to the public at large, and allows whoever may read his reports to use the results as they see fit. Voices are being raised proclaiming that he has responsibilities to do more than that, that he is obligated to protect the political interests of the subjects of his research.

Such a demand encounters formidable obstacles. It implies that the researcher has control of his findings; but he generally has little say about who uses his results or how. It implies, too, that perhaps he should censor certain information out of his reports, if it is susceptible to misuse by political antagonists. The suppression of evidence is contrary not only to scientific values but also to the human values we seek to protect.

It seems to me that the researcher can do three things:

a) Study issues of importance to the people who participate in the research in terms relevant to their concerns.

b) Make research findings available. There seems little justification for undertaking social-problem research under conditions that prevent full publication of results. The researcher may want to make special efforts to present his findings to the groups studied and help them use the research for the purposes they deem important. In cases of controversy, research data can be used by both sides. As Charles Kadushin recently noted,[8] this is the meaning of science.

c) Correct any misinterpretations that others make of his research. James Coleman, for example, challenged attempts to use his study as support for maintaining segregated schools. The American Association for Public Opinion Research, many of whose members do commercial research, has adopted an amendment to its code of ethics stating that "when misinterpretation [of our findings] appears, we shall publicly disclose what is required to correct it, notwithstanding our obligation for client confidentiality in all other respects."[9] Certainly, the researcher should speak out against abuses and clarify the import of his findings.

RESISTANCE OF RESEARCH SUBJECTS

This is a period of erosion of old authorities, perhaps not on the grand scale that professional viewers-with-alarm would have us believe, but certainly among critical segments of the young,

[8] Charles Kadushin, "Letter to the Editor," *Columbia Spectator*, January, 1970.
[9] American Association for Public Opinion Research, *Letter to Members*, June 25, 1970, pp. 2–3.

the minorities, and the radicals. Occasional spokesmen in these groups counsel resistance to social research. Unimpressed by promises of research's contributions to rational social policy, they question the homage that society expects for "science" and "research."

The poor and the black have never been excessively sympathetic to social research, partly because they could not understand the abstract processes by which it could make life better for them, partly because they felt undignified and helpless under its examination ("like guinea pigs" is the common phrase), and partly because of a distrust for the motives of the "power structure" that sponsored the research. In recent years there has been talk—and even some action—about encouraging the participation of local people in the research process. There have been experiments in community control of research, advocate-researchers employed by community groups, and the like. But for all the good intentions, research is still too esoteric and remote to seem truly useful to most slum residents. Moreover, they still see it as more likely to be hostile than supportive. There are some ghetto neighborhoods where wary suspicion has turned to outright noncooperation. No interviewer, black or white, is welcome.

White radicals, too, are increasingly suspicious of social research, and their criticism corroborates and tends to legitimate the old grievances. Radicals—some of them within the research professions—berate research for being handmaiden to the ruling militarists and imperialists. As we have noted, they question its motives and suspect its uses.

Columbia University's student newspaper *Columbia Spectator*, in January of 1970 urged students not to cooperate with an American Council on Education survey of student activities and opinions. One of the demands of Yale students in their May, 1970, demonstrations was that the university abandon a proposed institute of social research. Opposition of this sort, if it grows and spreads, can have doleful consequences. Today's occasional incidents of noncooperation can become frequent enough to paralyze research on controversial topics or among sensitive or embattled groups.

RESPONSE TO THE CHALLENGE

With more sensitivity for the rights of research subjects, the research fraternity can do much to overcome the ethical and political problems. Many steps have already been taken. To obtain grants from the National Institutes of Health and the National Institute of Mental Health, among others, all investigators who use human subjects must obtain the "informed consent" of their subjects; prospective subjects must be told enough about the research and its possible consequences to make an informed choice about whether or not to participate. Moreover, the institution for which the investigator works has the responsibility to review the consent procedures and safeguard the rights of subjects. It must provide for group review and decision by the researcher's peers, surveillance of procedures, and continuing advice to the investigator on the welfare of research subjects. The grantee institution is required to keep written records of group reviews and decisions on the use of human subjects and to keep documentary evidence of "informed consent." [10]

An influential report by the federal Office of Science and Technology warns against ignoring the rights of research subjects.[11] It discusses the trade-offs between the individual's right to privacy and society's right to discovery. In sober and sophisticated terms it recommends constant adjustment and compromise by weighing the cost and gains in each situation, the costs in privacy; the gains in knowledge. It recommends that the government support research only under conditions that give the fullest protection to human dignity. Consent and confidentiality are essential in all circumstances.

But with all the increased concern, much remains to be done. If we want to demonstrate that research is not a tool of the establishment, that emergent groups and anti-establishmentarians would do better to use it than undermine it, we shall have to give these groups genuine opportunities to participate in the research

---

[10] Katz, *op. cit.*; U.S. Department of Health, Education, and Welfare, Public Health Service, *Protection of the Individual as a Research Subject: Grants, Awards, Contracts* (Washington, D.C.: Government Printing Office, 1969).

[11] Executive Office of the President, *op. cit.*

process. Such participation can include: (1) reading the research report and drawing their own implications for action; (2) sitting down with the actual data and the researcher and threshing out the meaning and implications; (3) helping to develop the basic premises and direction of the study at the outset and then later participating in interpretation. Under given circumstances (studies of community needs, for example) any or all of these activities may be appropriate. When people have a say in the research, and can see its potential advantage to them, they are more likely to support it.

Today's movements of the black, the young, and other minorities need research just as research needs them. Dangerous currents of anti-intellectualism and disregard for social and historical facts are undermining their effectiveness. If we can help them make use of relevant and valid research, we all stand to gain. The concept of the advocate researcher—the professional researcher employed by, and responsible to, the "out"-group—deserves further trial.

I think we have a responsibility, too, as applied researchers, to do more research on institutions and systemic conditions rather than devoting all our time to analyzing the plight of the victims. Research on the old, the poor, the handicapped, the criminal, the illiterate, almost inevitably involves assumptions about *their* fault in the scheme of things: if only *they* would do something differently, the problems would be solved. Certainly we know enough to realize the overwhelming impact of social structures and social definitions, and their pathogenic features. It is time that our research programs, through a fairer division of emphasis, reflected this knowledge.

Finally, I think this is a time to exercise more restraint in the kinds of research that is done. Researchers have always operated within certain constraints. The selective availability of grant funds, for example, has led to neglect of some areas and the surge of interest in others. Our technical values have bid us forgo research of questionable methodology, for example, when time or funds are too short for competent work, and our social values have led us to avoid research that is requested for dubious purposes, such as delaying a decision and stalling action.

It is time that we recognize the values of research subjects as a constraining factor, and examine possible inquiries against the criterion of *their* welfare. We would do well to ask how a proposed study will affect *them*. Will it require them to sacrifice dignity, privacy, loyalties to family, friends, and social groups? Will study procedures differentiate them from others, label them as "undesirables," or in any way create harmful side effects? Will data on individuals or groups be recognizable enough to be used for purposes of control or retaliation? Are the study's theoretical assumptions consonant with the realities and pertinent to the interests of the group? What are the purposes of the study's sponsors? What uses do they anticipate making of the data? Are the results likely to be used to the disadvantage of the subject? Questions like these, which have not generally been considered in research reviews, deserve serious attention.

Moreover, the researcher's own judgment may not be enough protection for the subjects of his research. The ideal image of the researcher is an objective seeker after wisdom and truth, uninterested in worldly considerations and personal advantage. But the researcher has a stake in the situation. His interests involve doing his research.[12] While his motives may be of the highest—the advancement of knowledge, the betterment of the human condition—he cannot be an impartial arbiter between the competing values of knowledge and privacy.

Under these conditions, it becomes advisable to turn to the investigator's peers for further review. Much as the Surgeon General's regulations require consent procedures, the research organization might well provide group consideration and review of topics and methods of research inquiry, particularly in sensitive areas.

Outside censorship of research is intolerable. Responsible discussion and debate within the research community can help keep

[12] Forrest B. Tyler, "Shaping of the Science," *American Psychologist*, XXV (1970), 219–26.

human values to the fore and avoid the kinds of excesses that invite interference.

The group review must not degenerate into a logrolling operation—"You vote for my research and I'll vote for yours." It has to be a conscientious effort to protect the rights of participants. When supported by research peers, the researcher's institutional base, funding organizations, and the professions themselves, through codes of ethics, selection of papers for journal publication, and the operation of the professional reward system, the safeguarding of human values will become a salient factor.

Let us recognize that this will impose limits on the freedom of researchers. Some pet projects will not be done. Some of us are going to wax indignant. But if we reflect on how much research is done out of curiosity, voyeurism, habit, and rote, how little is related to core issues in our disciplines, and how few studies affect the making of social policy, we may be a little more humble. Surely there is enough significant research waiting to be done to keep all available talents engaged. At a time when dignity, privacy, and nonconformity are endangered as never before by the whole battery of technological advances in eavesdropping, recording, and data processing, by government attitudes, by public opinion, and by the sheer density of population, the claims of privacy and accountability deserve special weight.

Individualized Treatment of the Mentally Impaired Aged

ELAINE BRODY and
HERBERT A. SILVERMAN

THE MENTALLY IMPAIRED AGED are a population unmatched in their personal, social, and health deprivations and in the dismal nature of their prospects. That their future is dim is due in no small part to negative social attitudes and to the generally pervasive therapeutic pessimism which has characterized all professional disciplines, social work included, regarding their accessibility to treatment and their potential for improvement. Such attitudes result in deprivation not only of the psychological supports but of concrete supports such as facilities, programs, and services that are required to maximize social functioning.

For the past five years the Philadelphia Geriatric Center, under the leadership of Mr. Arthur Waldman, has been planning and implementing a concerted attack on the problems of this group.[1] The multitude of activities involved has been described elsewhere.[2] We shall deal here with one component of the process:

---

[1] The work described was made possible by NIMH grant #15047.
The authors are deeply indebted to Arthur Waldman, Executive Vice-president of the Philadelphia Geriatric Center, and Bernard Liebowitz, Assistant Executive Director, for their administrative support, encouragement, and creation of a climate in which such research-service activities can be carried out; to Dr. M. Powell Lawton and Dr. Morton Kleban for the generous and sophisticated application of their research expertise; to Charlotte Cole, project social worker, for her dedication and creative efforts on behalf of the project clients; and to those too numerous to be named—the staffs of the project and of the Home for the Jewish Aged in Philadelphia.

[2] See Arthur Waldman and M. Powell Lawton, "The Philadelphia Story," two lectures given in the University of Southern California series "Research Utilization in Mental Health of the Aging," 1970; Bernard Liebowitz and Elaine M. Brody,

a research investigation of a highly individualized program of service and treatment for a group of mentally impaired aged women residing in the Home for the Jewish Aged (HJA)[3] in Philadelphia. The project is now in its concluding phase.

The dimensions of the problem may be measured in part by the fact that people over sixty-five now constitute 10 percent of the population, or about 20 million individuals compared to about 4 percent of the population, or 3 million persons, at the turn of the century. As a group, they have less income and more mental and physical impairments than any other segment of the population. In addition, they are heir to a host of other problems: loss of spouse, peers, and adult children; loss of status, roles, and occupation. Within the total aging population, the very old are the most vulnerable. As the elderly individual moves toward advanced old age, he becomes progressively more likely to become a recipient of old age assistance,[4] requires hospital and medical care more frequently,[5] and is more likely to become institutionalized.[6] The suicide rate for elderly males is staggering.

For a particularly disadvantaged subgroup of old people, the insult of mental impairment has been added to the other injuries of aging. It has been estimated that about 20 percent of all people over sixty-five suffer from some form of mental impairment.[7] Of those, almost half, or more than 1.6 million individuals, suffer from severe manifestations of the particular form of mental im-

"Integration of Research and Practice in Creating a Continuum of Care for the Elderly," *Gerontologist*, X, No. 1, Part 1 (1970), 11–17.

[3] HJA is the 350-bed institutional facility of the Philadelphia Geriatric Center. The Center also includes two apartment buildings for the elderly (the York Houses), which house 500 residents, and the Gerontological Research Institute. HJA includes the hospital of HJA which is fully accredited by the Joint Commission on Hospital Accreditation. The full-time professional staff provides comprehensive medical, nursing, social work, recreational, occupational, and physical therapy, diagnostic laboratory, and X-ray services.

[4] Robert H. Mugge, "Age Variations in Old-Age Assistance," *Welfare in Review*, IV, No. 40 (1966), 13–18.

[5] Jack Scharff, "Current Medicare Survey: the Medical Insurance Sample," *Social Security Bulletin*, XXX, No. 4 (1967), 4–9.

[6] Herman D. Brotman, "Who Are the Aged?—a Demographic View," in *Useful Facts*, #22 (Washington, D.C.: Administration on Aging, U.S. Department of Health, Education, and Welfare, 1968; mimeographed).

[7] Group for the Advancement of Psychiatry, *Psychiatry and the Aged: an Introductory Approach*, Report No. 59 (New York: the Group), 1965.

Treatment of the Mentally Impaired Aged

pairment commonly described as "senility."[8] "Mental impairment" in this context is used in relation to organic brain disorders characterized by a relatively permanent deficit in the capacity of intellectual functioning with symptoms such as confusion, impairment of orientation, memory, perception, knowledge, and judgment.[9] Since the ailment is somewhat age-linked, occurring more often among those over eighty-five, and since the number of those over eighty-five is increasing at a rate more than double that of the total population over sixty-five,[10] it is obvious that the problem will grow.

A simple head count of this group does not reflect the full impact of the problem, which is felt by all members of each generation in the family and by all of society. This is one of the most socially disruptive of all medical-psychiatric problems. Forgetfulness and confusion may be manifested in behavior which disrupts the life of the family and even endangers the old person and those around him. The tendency to leave gas burners aflame, the practice of wandering and getting lost, poor habits of personal hygiene, nighttime wakefulness, unsanitary housekeeping conditions, eccentric and embarrassing social behavior—the litany of symptoms is long. Deficits in ability to perform functions of personal self-care and the need for close and constant supervision make heavy demands on the time and energy of other people. The social and emotional cost to families may be counted not only in the economic currency of financial stress but in the coin of physical and emotional strain, loss of time from work, constraints on the ability to take vacations or engage in normal social and recreational activities, strain on interpersonal relationships, and deprivations suffered by the youngest generation in the family constellation.

---

[8] Alvin I. Goldfarb, "The 'Senile' Older Person," in *Selected Papers, Fifth Annual National Conference of State Executives on Aging* (Washington, D.C.: U.S. Department of Health, Education, and Welfare, 1965), pp. 42–45.

[9] Arthur P. Noyes, M.D., and Lawrence C. Kalb, M.D., *Modern Clinical Psychiatry* (Philadelphia: W. B. Saunders Co., 1958), p. 170.

[10] George W. Grier, "Goals and Objectives in Aging," in *Creating Opportunities for Older Persons*, selected papers from the Fourth Annual Conference of State Executives on Aging (Washington, D.C.: Department of Health, Education, and Welfare, 1964).

While there are large concentrations of these sick old people in institutions of all types, most of them are in the community. Their neglect both in and out of institutions has been well documented. Social workers are familiar with the pressing need for protective services; with the back wards of psychiatric hospitals which in many instances are not much more than warehouses overstocked with human inventory considered obsolescent; with the lack of appropriate facilities so that sick old people live in substandard nursing or boarding homes, or barely subsist in the community under conditions to which human beings should not be consigned.

What is abundantly clear is that the plight of this group is a major social problem requiring the concentrated attention of practitioners, researchers, social planners, government, and the citizenry. It delineates a situation of the deepest poignancy that claims our values and skills as social workers.

What is known about mental impairment? For our purposes, one fact stands out: there is no one-to-one simplistic relationship between the extent of organic impairment and the over-all disturbance of the individual's functioning. Extensive organic changes may take place without severe behavioral changes; conversely, severe disturbances of behavior can occur with relatively mild brain tissue pathology.[11] As Corsellis states in his classic work, "human behavior is fortunately a great deal more subtle than the science of neuropathology." [12]

Since organic changes alone do not explain the functioning level, it is necessary to look further. Clinical and experimental evidence supports the view that the individual's functioning is also influenced by a variety of physical, psychological, social, and cultural factors. Among the factors hypothesized as contributing to the manifestations of mental impairment are physical illness,[13]

[11] David Rothschild and M. L. Sharp, "The Origin of Senile Psychoses: Neuropathologic Factors of a More Personal Nature," *Diseases of the Nervous System*, II (1941), 49.

[12] J. A. N. Corsellis, *Mental Illness and the Aging Brain* (London: Oxford University Press, 1962).

[13] Marjorie F. Lowenthal, *Lives in Distress* (New York: Basic Books, 1964); Alvin Goldfarb, "Prevalence of Psychiatric Disorders in Metropolitan Old Age and Nursing Homes," *Journal of the American Geriatric Society*, X (1962), 77–84.

which is highly correlated with mental impairment; the "life crises" of aging which constitute stresses that precipitate or intensify mental deterioration; [14] the premorbid personality; [15] previous modes of adaptation to stress; [16] and adverse environmental conditions.[17] Inevitably, the interaction of all these factors has been suggested as accounting for the range in behavioral variations.[18]

Prior to this project, there had been attempts to treat the mentally impaired elderly through creation of a therapeutic milieu [19] and by group occupational and social therapeutic techniques.[20] The positive impact of these programs was short-lived when the stimuli were removed. However, the fact that the subjects did not continue activities after the stimulus of the worker was withdrawn is not to say that the programs "failed." Lawton

[14] Irving Rosow, "Adjustment of the Normal Aged," in Richard Hayes Williams, Clark Tibbetts, and Wilma Donahue, eds., *Processes of Aging* (New York: Atherton Press, 1963), pp. 195–223.

[15] Sidney L. Sands and David Rothschild, "Foundations for a Theory of the Reactions to Aging," *Journal of Nervous and Mental Diseases*, CXVI (1952), 223.

[16] Robert S. Kahn, Max Pollack, and Alvin Goldfarb, "Factors Related to Individual Differences in Mental Status of Institutionalized Aged," in Paul Hoch and Joseph Zubin, eds., *Psychopathology of Aging* (New York: Grune and Stratton, 1961), pp. 104–13.

[17] Leo Chalfen, "Leisure-Time Adjustment of the Aged II: Activities and Interests and Some Factors Influencing Choice," *Journal of Genetic Psychology*, LXXXVIII (1956), 261–76; Robert W. Kleemeier, "The Use and Meaning of Time in Special Settings: Retirement Communities, Homes for the Aged, Hospitals, and Other Group Settings," in Kleemeier, ed., *Aging and Leisure: a Research Perspective into the Meaningful Use of Time* (New York: Oxford University Press, 1961), pp 273–308; Ruth Laverty, "Nonresident Aid—Community versus Institutional Care for Older People," *Journal of Gerontology*, V (1950), 370–74.

[18] Leonard E. Gottesman, "Problems in Assessing Determinants of Normal and Pathological Aging" (Ann Arbor: University of Michigan, Division of Gerontology, 1963).

[19] Joseph Sklar and Francis J. O'Neil, "Experiments with Intensive Treatment in a Geriatric Ward," in Hoch and Zubin, *op. cit.*, pp. 266–73; Irving Wolf, Joseph M. Sacks, and Aaron S. Mason, "A Research Treatment Program for Geriatric Mental Patients," *Journal of Gerontology*, XIV (1959), 469–72; Wilma Donahue *et al.*, "Rehabilitation of Geriatric Patients in County Hospitals—a Preliminary Report," *Geriatrics*, XV (1960), 263–74; Leonard E. Gottesman and Peter T. Schneider, "The Interactions of Opportunity, Mental Status, and Attitudes in the Adjustment of Geriatric Mental Patients," Social Science Research Seminar, Markaryd, Sweden, 1963.

[20] Lionel Z. Cosin *et al.*, "Persistent Senile Confusion: Study of 50 Consecutive Cases," *International Journal of Social Psychiatry*, III (1957) 195–202, IV (1958), 24–42.

raises this basic issue: "May a program not be judged as successful simply by virtue of the fact that activities are performed, without insisting that the improvement be self-maintaining?" [21] Why *should* we so insist? The diabetic and the cardiac require lifetime health care, as do those who suffer from a host of other ailments. The chronicity of mental impairment also indicates a need for long-term service and treatment.

In general, previous treatment programs began with patients who were existing at a much lower level of adequacy of care than is offered at the HJA. In effect, then, this project stacked the cards against itself in two ways: our subjects were already receiving sophisticated care and therefore were less likely to have untreated conditions which affected functioning negatively; and they represented a population which in general has been "written off" as inaccessible to treatment.

Our project undertook to tailor treatment to the unique requirements of each individual as well as to his social environment, to tackle the research complexities of the interaction of multiple sources of disability, and to focus the organization and delivery of services by using the concept of "excess disability." This key concept of "excess disability" (a term coined by Kahn) [22] highlights the discrepancy which exists when the individual's functional incapacity is greater than that warranted by the actual impairment. In short, it denotes the gap between actual function and potential function. We assumed that the excess disabilities were attributable to physical, psychological, and/or social factors and that they could exist in any or all of those spheres. They were specified as "excess" if deemed amenable to treatment intervention. The ultimate goal was functional improvement.

Four basic premises guided our thinking:

1. Each person is unique. The problems suffered by the elderly individual, his adaptations, the disabilities under which he la-

[21] M. Powell Lawton, "Planning a Building for the Mentally Impaired Aged" (Philadelphia: Philadelphia Geriatric Center, 1966; mimeographed).

[22] Robert S. Kahn, "Comments," in *Proceedings of the York House Institute on the Mentally Impaired Aged* (Philadelphia: Philadelphia Geriatric Center, 1965), pp. 109-14.

Treatment of the Mentally Impaired Aged

bors, the feelings he manifests, the responses he evidences and those he elicits from others, grow out of the unique soil of a highly differentiated lifetime. Accordingly, any program of treatment must take into consideration his unique requirements, strengths, and deficits.

2. As is characteristic of the elderly, the physical, mental, and social disabilities are clustered and interact so as to mask and exacerbate each other. Treatment in each sphere, therefore, should be specific and clear, yet so integrated as to focus on the whole man. This implied the necessity for a multidisciplinary treatment team based on the concept of the unity and the integrity of each human individual.

3. Enhanced functioning is the objective of treatment. Impairments in each sphere were therefore perceived not in isolation, but in terms of the impact of that condition on the individual's over-all functioning as a social being. Since the environment (personal, social, and physical) affects functioning, it too was considered a legitimate object of treatment.

4. Treatment goals should be consonant with the characteristics of the target population. Therefore, global objectives appropriate to other groups, such as discharge from institution, resumption of paid employment or household management, were not realistic for our subjects. Gains were to be measured in more "molecular" terms, such as movement from wheelchair to walker, or from total apathy to some level of social participation.

Criteria for selection of HJA residents for inclusion in the project were:

1. Moderate to severe mental impairment (established by administration of the Kahn-Goldfarb-Pollack Mental Status Questionnaire and confirmed by the project physician)

2. Freedom from known illness that would be fatal within a year (established via judgment of the physician on the basis of a thorough medical examination)

3. Freedom from a history of functional psychosis prior to age sixty

4. A minimum of three months of residence in HJA (to avoid the difficulties of the initial adjustment period).

The study was limited to females, since too few men met the criteria to permit adequate male representation in the final sample.

Thirty-two pairs of women were matched on the basis of their mental status scores and physical classification scores [23] and assigned randomly to experimental and control groups. The subjects in both groups remained in their usual accommodations, interspersed among other residents on two floors of the institution. Each subject was given a thorough clinical evaluation by the multidisciplinary team and was rated on a group of rating and measuring instruments. A year of planned and closely coordinated treatment by the project staff ensued for the experimental subjects; the controls continued to receive the usual high-level services provided by HJA. During that year, midpoint team reevaluation reviewed progress of the subjects and reformulated goals and assignments if necessary; if significant events occurred in their lives the team convened for the same purpose. For the final evaluation, the same complete individual assessment was given to both the control and the experimental group and the subjects' status was reviewed to determine any changes in the previously identified excess disabilities.

Intensive and thoroughgoing review and evaluation of the individual subject were fundamental to defining the problems and deciding upon the appropriate treatment. Therefore, a great deal of preliminary care and thought went into the development of a social history, protocols for recording clinical data, and scales to rate the subject along medical, psychological, social, and detailed behavioral dimensions.[24]

Each member of the team, which included social work, nursing, medicine, psychiatry, recreational therapy, and physiotherapy, was responsible for gathering and evaluating the information relevant to his expertise. The excess disabilities were identified by consen-

---

[23] The classification scheme used in this study has been in use at HJA for several years. It serves to indicate the level of medical care and supervision required by the subject. See Arthur Waldman and Evelyn Fryman, "Classification in Homes for the Aged," in Herbert H. Shore and Morton Leeds, eds., *Geriatric Institutional Management* (New York: Putnam's, 1965), pp. 131–35.

[24] Instruments are available from the authors on request.

Treatment of the Mentally Impaired Aged

sus of the multidisciplinary staff at the team meeting, and the accessibility to treatment of the conditions pinpointed were considered in the light of the subject's assets and deficits.

Once a disability was specified as "excess," it became the object of a planned, coordinated, and integrated program of treatment. Each member of the multidisciplinary team whose skill was appropriate to treatment of the denoted excess disability was given specific tasks relative to the condition. It was intended that the separate activities of the team would reinforce each other in the planned treatment program. A master chart was developed to enable us to outline in a concise and ordered manner the disabilities to be treated, the responsibilities of each team member, and the specific goals. It also served to control and coordinate the treatment plan and to measure progress.

Case vignettes illustrate the application of the underlying concepts of the experimental treatment approach, that is, the individualization of the subject, integration of multidisciplinary treatment, and the focus on excess disability:

Mrs. A. Eighty-one-year-old Mrs. A. spent her days sitting in the hallway and carrying on conversations with hallucinatory images. She ignored other residents and was content to relate to staff only to the extent of meeting her basic needs. The social history revealed that in a long and unhappy life she suffered a great deal of self-denial, disparagement by her siblings, and a childless marriage to a very limited husband. Only two bright spots were noted in her history. First, she was very close to one of her nieces, who continued to show devotion to her by making frequent visits and bringing gifts. Second, she had been an excellent cook. The staff perceived these facts as providing a likely entry point to involving Mrs. A. in an activity with social content. The lack of activity with real social involvement was seen as an "excess disability." Accordingly, the niece was recruited as a volunteer to supervise the cooking activities of Mrs. A. and of other residents who might be interested. The project social worker arranged with the administrator and the food-service manager to gain access to kitchen facilities during off hours. Under her niece's stimulation and supervision, Mrs. A. resumed the practice of her culinary art and chatted with residents in the group. The occupational therapist recorded the recipes she dictated, and Mrs. A. watched her personal recipe book grow with pride and anticipation. She enjoyed having her cookies sampled.

Mrs. B. Depressed and complaining, this 86-year-old woman criticized everything to anyone who would listen, and was not involved in any activity. The staff denoted her depression and complaining behavior as "excess disabilities" and aimed to provide more environmental stimulation. It was learned from her children that Mrs. B. had been a socialist activist and enjoyed keeping up with current events. Accordingly, a subscription was obtained to a socialist newspaper in her native language. Soon, Mrs. B. was reading it regularly and avidly and delighted in sharing her comments on world and local political and social events. She was enrolled in the occupational therapy program, which she attended four days each week. Because of her poor memory, she had to be reminded of her scheduled activities by the occupational therapy worker. When this was done, Mrs. B. would find her own way to the occupational therapy room. There was a notable improvement in the manner of her interaction with the staff and socialization with other residents and a discernible lifting of her depression.

Mrs. C. Mrs. C., age 79, was slightly over five feet tall and weighed over two hundred pounds. She had a long history of orthopedic difficulty beginning in 1954 when she was involved in an automobile accident. A spinal disc was removed in 1965 to prevent complete immobilization. Unable to walk after the surgery, she spent two months in a rehabilitation hospital after which she was ambulatory with the assistance of two canes. Transferred to a private nursing home, she was unhappy there and regressed to the point of being confined to a wheelchair. After admission to HJA, Mrs. C. was again referred to the rehabilitation hospital, where she was fitted with a brace and received training in the use of a quad cane. When she went back to the Home she complained of the pain and returned again to her wheelchair. At the time that Mrs. C. was selected for the project, the wheelchair was her only form of locomotion. While the pain was real, it was aggravated by her obesity and edema of the legs. Despite her apparent resignation to a passive state, confinement to the wheelchair was frustrating to Mrs. C., who had a lifelong pattern of independence. She defended against the anxiety this created by a bitter humor, and an underlying depression was also noted. Her real capacity for enjoyment of social contacts was restricted by the confinement to the wheelchair, and she was therefore unable to partake of entertainment and social events to the degree she would have liked. The lack of ambulation, depression, and social isolation were noted as excess disabilities.

Medical evaluation indicated that there was no physical reason that Mrs. C. could not walk. However, two physical conditions had to be relieved. First, a diet was required to reduce her weight in order to

Treatment of the Mentally Impaired Aged

lessen the pain in her arthritic knee. A complicating factor was the fact that Mrs. C.'s children brought her food when they visited. The social worker conferred with the children to explain the project goals for their mother and to elicit their cooperation. The cooperation was given and maintained. The prescribed diet was changed, and nursing supervision over Mrs. C.'s food intake was tightened. Secondly, the edematous legs were treated by daily Jobst boot treatments administered by the physical therapist.

The social worker stoked Mrs. C.'s motivational fires. On a twice-daily schedule, he helped Mrs. C. practice her walking and encouraged her to tolerate the pain that was inevitable in the early stages. The distance covered each time was noted, and her weight was recorded weekly. All this was put into graphic form so that Mrs. C. could see her progress pictorially. The social worker and Mrs. C. walking down the hall became such a familiar sight to the other residents that they took to making encouraging comments. At one point, Mrs. C. mentioned that, between the loss of weight and the increasing ability to walk, she looked forward to putting on a corset, a nice dress, and walking to meals like a *mensch*—a *person*.

IMPLICATIONS FOR SOCIAL WORK

The philosophy of this project, the hypotheses on which it rested, and the methods utilized were entirely consonant with social work knowledge and goals. Social work traditionally has been concerned with the "whole man" as an individual and in his reciprocal relations with his family, environment, and society. The commitment of our profession is to maximize social functioning of all individuals, regardless of race, handicap, or age. No claim is made that the social work component of the study was innovative. We simply attempted to exploit to the fullest extent the experience and techniques of the field.

The social workers functioned as direct-service practitioners and as interpreters of behavior, mobilizers and coordinators of resources and personnel, enablers and advocates for clients and family, and change-agents in the institutional community. Treatment goals were calibrated to a level appropriate to the potential of the clients. Social work activities were carried out in the context of thoroughly integrated collaborative efforts with all "significant others" in the environment—nurses, aides, food-service personnel, occupational and recreational therapists, physiotherapist, housekeepers, as well as the traditional team of physician, psychologist, and psychiatrist. Social services were directed not only to the individuals and their families, but toward modification of the environment when necessary. The intimate study of the elderly people led naturally to some understanding of how the environment, in terms of personnel, routines, programs, activities, attitudes, could respond to their needs and thus support function.

One of the more satisfying aspects of the project was its exemplification of the way in which service and research can and do enrich each other. Both were utilized in developing the research design, constructing and testing the instruments, and gathering and organizing the research data to capitalize on their clinical implications. The need of research for precise information served to sharpen the clinical tools used for diagnosis and treatment. Thus, the information was gathered systematically, and treatment goals were made explicit. At the same time, the clinical experiences fed back to the researchers any shortcomings in their instruments. Currently, as findings are being analyzed, research and practice are collaborating in interpreting the data.

We have stated elsewhere that "the practitioner, because of his direct observations of human needs and problems, the paths which led to them and the unavailable remedies, occupies a vantage point for the identification of questions which should and could be researched. To be useful for planning, the practitioners' knowledge must be retrieved, systematized, and tested via research so that it can be translated into policy and program." [25] In Alvin Schorr's words, "apart from the basic commitment of social work that practice represents, it is also the foundation for those who would influence social policy. Decisions about social policy ought to rest on data, after all." [26]

When results from this project are available, they will be implemented at the host institution. These efforts will have a firm foundation in the data which evaluated the impact of the services. It is hoped that communication of our findings to the field

[25] Liebowitz and Brody, *op. cit.*
[26] Alvin L. Schorr, Editorial, *Social Work*, No. 3 (1966), 2.

will stimulate other congregate care facilities to make positive changes in their programming.

It is gratifying to report that the preliminary data indicate that the experimental subjects showed significantly greater improvements in their excess disabilities than did those in the control group.[27] Detailed data analysis will allow us to answer questions such as: How did the positive changes in excess disabilities affect the individual's over-all functioning? What were the predictors of improvement or lack of improvement?[28] Which treatments were most effective?

An additional study has been designed to continue longitudinal observation of the same individuals. It poses questions such as: What are the longer-range effects, if any, of the treatment program after project treatment has ceased? What is the course of mental impairment and adaptation to it over time? Can close observation establish predictors and patterns which presage death?

Though positive, the results of this project will not provide a panacea. We expect that the unanswered questions will far exceed in number those that we may be able to answer. Many issues will be raised which may provide clues for subsequent investigations and investigators. However, at the very least, we can claim a positive impact. What this means is that *something can be done*. Social work and the other professions can approach this problem positively.

As social workers, we need not await scientific breakthroughs which prevent or "cure" this form of mental impairment; for we have not in the past withheld our skills and efforts while waiting for scientific breakthroughs to cure ulcers, prevent amputations, control schizophrenia, or for social changes to eliminate poverty and discrimination. The mentally impaired aged, then, are legitimate recipients of our services. Whether in the microcosm of the institutional community or in the macrocosm of the general com-

[27] Elaine M. Brody, Herbert A. Silverman, and Morton H. Kleban, "Impact of Individualized Treatment of Mentally Impaired Aged," Annual Scientific Meeting of the Gerontological Society, Toronto, Canada, 1970.

[28] Morton H. Kleban, Elaine M. Brody, and Herbert Silverman, "Personality Traits in the Mentally Impaired Aged and Their Relationship to Improvements in Current Functioning," Annual Scientific Meeting of the Gerontological Society, Toronto, Canada, 1970.

munity, social work can share, if it will, contributions to the sadly needed technology for the treatment of this neglected group and participate in effecting the social changes required to remove them from their status as "untouchables." Gerontologists have emphasized consistently that the well-being of the generations is interlocked socially, economically, and psychologically. If we abdicate our responsibility to the mentally impaired aged, the effect will be to disadvantage this and all future generations.

A Social Service Team for Public Welfare

HARRIS CHAIKLIN

THE COMMUNITY ORGANIZATION AND SERVICES to Improve Family Living Project is a rarity; it was designed to test an innovative staff service delivery pattern for working with public welfare families.[1] This is not done very often. Edward E. Schwartz, who with William C. Sample conducted an experiment on ways of retaining and effectively using public welfare manpower, says:

> A review of the literature on social welfare manpower and observation of the efforts of the social work profession and of social welfare organizations to deal with it revealed the almost exclusive focus on staff recruitment and training to the almost total neglect of considerations of staff retention and utilization.[2]

The problem is deeper than simple neglect or overemphasis of a few manpower components. The rediscovery of poverty has made public welfare policy an intense and respectable public issue. Public welfare departments and what they do are accorded no such acceptance. Many oppose any efforts to improve services because they consider reform as a disguised effort to continue oppressing the poor. The most powerful argument advanced by this line of reasoning is that services are no substitute for money. The

---

[1] This was project D-217 funded as a demonstration in public assistance under Section 1115 of the Social Security Act of 1962, as amended. It ran from June 1, 1967, to June 30, 1970, and was conducted by the Community Relations Division of the Baltimore City Department of Social Services. Special thanks are given to my silent co-authors: Geraldine Aronin, Chief of Community Relations; Barbara Mikulski, Assistant Chief of Community Relations; Bette Stein, Project Director; and Gary Balzer, Casework Supervisor.

[2] Edward E. Schwartz, "The Field Experiment: Background, Plans, and Selected Findings," *Social Service Review*, XLI (1967), 115.

report of the President's Commission on Income Maintenance Programs makes the point eloquently:

> The broadening of social services has not led to a reduction in welfare. In fact, some of the largest increases in welfare rolls have occurred since 1962, despite consistent economic gains for the general population. This suggests that the appropriate roles of services and cash income maintenance have been confused. There is no evidence that services—particularly the counseling services generally provided by welfare departments—are effective in the absence of basic income. It has been suggested, moreover, that the compulsory nature of social services may reduce the effectiveness of those services, because clients resist being labeled social problems and are unable to develop rapport with a caseworker with whom they also must argue over money. . . . In attempting to choose between providing the poor with increments of service or income, we find that insufficient data exist to guide a definitive choice. However, we do know that the incidence of various social problems decreases as income increases. And no evidence suggests that current social services are effective or would be effective on an expanded basis without increased incomes.[3]

Eloquence, however, is no substitute for facts. This statement is little more than an attempt to kill off services with an American form of economic determinism. We do not know that social pathology decreases as income increases. As income increases, people change their deviance and/or become more astute at hiding what is socially disapproved; poor people are seldom indicted for embezzlement, and poor pregnant girls are not able to visit a distant aunt and obtain an "appendectomy." When you are hungry you must have bread before services mean anything; that is different from putting service and income on a mutually exclusive basis.[4]

The need for adequate services is an independent variable for rich and poor alike. Simply adding money to an existing system without changing patterns of service delivery does not really

---

[3] *Poverty amid Plenty: the American Paradox*, report of the President's Commission on Income-Maintenance Programs (Washington, D.C.: U.S. Government Printing Office, 1969), pp. 140–41.

[4] For an analysis of this proposition see Harris Chaiklin, "Motivating the Poor," in Benjamin Schlesinger, ed., *Poverty in Canada and the United States* (Toronto: University of Toronto Press, 1966), pp. 3–13.

help. A dramatic example of the results of this approach exists in the area of medical care. In 1968 $3.7 billion was expended on Medicare; the 1969 estimate is $4.6 billion; and the 1970 estimate, $5.8.[5] The nearly unanimous verdict on this financial flood is that our medical care system is a shambles and on the verge of collapse. What happened? Few would deny that the principles on which Medicare is based are sound, or that the struggle to enact the program represents one of the better moments in American social welfare history. But all the effort went into the campaign, and little attention was paid to possible ramifications within the medical care system.

There is no doubt that if they had more money, the majority of public welfare recipients would put it to excellent use. It is equally true, as the President's Commission implies, that if more money were given and all services eliminated, there would be a catastrophe in the alternate support systems which are available when the community has to intervene in a person's life. There are simply too many people now receiving public welfare who need service.

What is needed is to be able to say how much money people need and how much service they need. To do this requires the slow, patient work of building accountability systems. At present, this is not popular. Now the demand is for "action" and "relevance." These terms have become trite and desiccated through overuse. By refusing to look at what is going on in public welfare departments the policy pontificators are able to paint utopian pictures about what will happen when their revolutionary new plan is adopted.

Günter Grass in his novel *Local Anaesthetic* uses two major characters, a dentist and a high school teacher, to dissect exquisitely the way in which "action's" meaning has become convo-

[5] Martin Rein, "Choice and Change in the American Welfare System," *Annals*, 385 (1969), 89–109. By ways of contrast, the report of the President's Commission on Income Maintenance Programs (p. 115) places the 1968 federal share of all categorical aids at $3.1 billion. Of this total the federal share of AFDC was $0.5 billion and the combined federal and state total for AFDC was $2.8 billion. In other words 8 million AFDC recipients depended for almost their total livelihood on an amount equal to about two thirds of the amount expended for Medicare.

luted. In this passage the dentist begins by advising the teacher not to call the police about the threatened illegal actions of a student:

"Look who wants to call in the guardians of the law. Keep up your dialogue with the boy. Dialogue prevents action."
Me an accomplice of law and order! He treats everything like caries: "Prevention is the cure. Not revolution but dental prophylaxis. Treatment at the preschool age. Campaigns against sucking and against breathing through the mouth. Blowing exercises to combat distal bite. Too much action, too many one-eyed victories grabbing at the mood when there is still no effective toothpaste. Too many men of action, too many knot cutters."
Can it be that action is active resignation? Something is trying to develop; it moves ever so slightly, and there comes your man of action and bashes in the hothouse windows. "Then you deny that fresh air is beneficial?"
"Interrupting a process of development whose early stages gave ground for hope . . ." [sic]
Action as evasion. Something has got to happen. The agent, a juridical concept. What does it mean to gird for action, to convert something into action? If my dentist wants to prevent action by dialogue, he must believe that dialogue is not action. I remember what he said when he first saw my tartar: "Looks bad. We'll have to remove it radically." What if I liken capitalism to this tartar that has to be removed?
And even so. What about my dentist's assault on my prognathism which he called congenital and therefore authentic? Wasn't that action? He will say: Knowledge plus skill, whereas the precipitate extraction of teeth, this mania for creating gaps that no longer hurt, is action without knowledge; active stupidity.
Therefore hard work, doubt, reason, the acquisition of more knowledge, new beginnings, scarcely perceptible improvement, mistakes allowed for in the over-all plan, step-by-step evolution: two steps forward and one back; whereas your man of action skips the intervening steps, rejects the knowledge that would slow him down; he is light-footed and lazy; laziness is the promoter of action.[6]

While Grass continues at some length, his main point is clear: the teacher, who fancies himself a revolutionary, was going to use action as "active resignation," or "evasion," or "active stupidity,"

[6] Günter Grass, tr. Ralph Manheim, *Local Anaesthetic* (New York: Harcourt, Brace & World, Inc., 1969), pp. 151–53.

A Social Service Team for Public Welfare

or as a form of "laziness" while the dentist, who is portrayed as a prototype organization man, wants to take the active step of preventing precipitate action by "dialogue" and is willing to take his chances with action based on "knowledge." Would that we had the same spirit among those who seek to determine public welfare policy.

Those who demand instant solutions to public welfare problems have no time to find out what really works. They use the demand for action as a way of avoiding action. They cannot see that some form of public services, both social and emotional, will always be necessary no matter how much money is provided or under what auspices. This has been the experience of every welfare state. Social, economic, and political changes create new classes of disadvantaged people at a faster pace than the system can change to meet their needs.

The poor cannot wait until those with the miraculous solutions conclude their endless policy debate. An improvement in the material and social-emotional life of people on public welfare is desperately needed. It is going to come only from understanding and using our present system as a base from which to make changes. This holds for even the most radical changes. As Harry Hopkins said in a classic exchange between himself and a senator who wanted to wait and see if any antidepression programs were really needed: "The unemployed are hungry and miserable *now* . . . and business statistics aren't going to fill their bellies tomorrow or pay next week's rest. People don't eat in the long run, Senator, they eat every day." [7]

Most social welfare professionals know this. Yet they have resisted being active in the struggle to determine public welfare policy. Profound statements which are on the right side of an issue, when it is too late to influence the outcome, are not really part of the process of policy determination. Policy is determined by those who win the struggle to have their goals take precedence over competing aims. It is a matter of setting and sticking to priorities. And what is the nature of priority determination? John Lindsay provides a succinct answer: "Where there are priorities

[7] Cabell Phillips, *1929–1939* (New York: New York Times Co., 1969), pp. 264–65.

there is politics."[8] Those who work for public agencies cannot engage in politics, at least overtly. They can do a better job of documenting what they do and showing what their needs are. They can do more to show when they are doing the best possible job and what are the limits under which they work.

This is what is innovative about the Family Living Project. It was not designed to find a quick way to close cases but rather to take large families with a low potential for rehabilitation and by applying modest increments of cash and services explore ways to help people help themselves achieve more stable patterns of family living. The project's major concern was with supplementing rent payments, bringing housing up to code standards, and changing ineffective patterns of family behavior.

Over its three-year life the project served 280 families, representing 1,889 individuals. The selection criteria included all families who lived in a specified geographical target area, who were currently receiving Aid to Families with Dependent Children (AFDC) payments, had no father in the home, were not living in public housing, and had four or more children.

Financial increments were a variable (range $0–$54) rent supplement, a monthly family social participation allowance of $5 and, during the last year of the project, a variable ($0–$16) utility bill supplement. The combined rent and utility supplement could not exceed $54. There were one-time payments in the following categories: $30 to turn on utilities; up to $125 for furniture; and up to $25 for moving expenses. The total of all financial increments allocated amounted to less than a 15 percent increase in a family's budget. It moved them from roughly 50 percent below nationally defined poverty standards to approximately 40 percent below these standards.

The operating arm of the project was the service team, consisting of caseworkers, community organizers, and family aides. The service focus was on family as well as individual needs. Each of these job titles is familiar; even combining them into a service team is not unique. What is exceptional is that this exploration of the relationship between staffing models and the effectiveness of service delivery occurred in a public welfare setting.

[8] John V. Lindsay, "The Plight of the Cities," *Progressive*, XXXIV (1970), 29–31.

Normal staffing for 280 AFDC families would be four social workers and four fifths of a supervisor. The project had a director, a supervisor, five caseworkers, three community organizers, and five family aides. Caseworkers' assignments were dropped from seventy-five to fifty families.

The real staff increment came from the addition of the community organizers and the family aides. The presence of a project director facilitated administrative control. Decreasing the caseworkers' assignments did not represent an actual work reduction since a regular AFDC caseload would not have this number of large families and the additional problems which show up when greater numbers of people are served.

Other features of the project were direct telephone access and a decentralized office. Early fears about being inundated by telephone calls and walk-ins never materialized. The reverse was true; once clients found that they could reach the office easily, they tended to make contact only when there was a real need.

The team in action made it possible to offer project families material, service, and educational opportunities not ordinarily available to AFDC families. It did this while meeting all other aspects of agency policy requirements other than those changes already identified.

The caseworkers coordinated the team around meeting family needs. They did best at identifying reality needs and in seeing that effective follow-up procedures were instituted and carried out. When families needed intensive casework treatment, they found that community resources were scarce and that they did not have the necessary skills to carry out such work themselves. This was frustrating to the staff, but the lack of personality treatment skills is to be found in almost any welfare department in the country. Schwartz and Sample report a similar occurrence in the Midway project.[9]

Each community organizer was responsible for a different service sector. These included: (1) housing and legal services; (2) health; and (3) education, recreation, and employment. The community organizers located or initiated a truly amazing range of services and material resources for families. There was consulta-

[9] "First Findings from Midway," *Social Service Review*, XLI (1967), 113–51.

tion with landlords on housing problems. About 30 percent of all housing complaints were handled through these consultations. One landlord wrote the department that he had had welfare clients in his houses for twenty-five years, but this was the first time anybody from the welfare department had ever asked him anything. Where there was no compliance from the landlord, the project followed up with formal complaints to appropriate city authorities. In cooperation with the University of Maryland Dental School's Department of Community Dentistry a preventive dentistry program was developed. Until a combination of factors forced suspension of this program, the clinic "show rate" for these families, who everyone "knew" were not interested in preventive care, was better than that in the regular clinic where people come because of emergent dental problems. Legal aid services for everything from family difficulties to consumer protection, were used by almost half the project families. During the first year the project discovered that under the Elementary and Secondary Education Art funds were available for school clothes. The project used the entire allotment. The next year, when the school system had accepted the idea of using these funds, the project families had to share this resource with other families. This listing of services is only illustrative of the kinds of activities developed by the staff.

Public and private services and resources are underutilized because the work loads of public welfare caseworkers are so heavy that they do not have time to explore these possibilities. Whenever public welfare clients cannot get services which are available and to which they are entitled, they lose and the community loses. If this project had accomplished nothing else it would have been worthwhile for the clarity with which it demonstrated that community organizers have a service function in a public agency.

The family aides are women with much experience in the art of living. They have lived their lives close to the poverty line. Through in-service training they developed the ability to communicate their knowledge to others. Having the aides in the service team was important in helping many families develop a capability for utilizing the additional resources available to them.

A Social Service Team for Public Welfare

They were invaluable in working with mothers on budgeting and shopping matters and in cooperating with the community organizers to get a mothers' group functioning.

This was the team. What did it accomplish? In terms of bare statistics, it is apparent that much was done. During the second year of the project the rent supplement averaged $30 a month per family. The need for rental funds was being met. This does not say much, however. These families pay more for rent than their housing is worth, but few of them moved where they could take advantage of the full supplement because adequate housing was often not available and/or they did not want to face being forced to move again when the project ended.

The families' housing was in better shape as a result of the project. Between the first and second year the number of major defects, such as plumbing and electrical, dropped from 218 to 116. Given the age of inner city housing, housing deterioration will continue. Code enforcement cannot make a house which is old beyond its time adequate. Vigorous enforcement can see that the houses are kept livable by making sure that repairs are handled promptly.

Family life was improved for these families, but major psychosocial problems continued to occur as rapidly as they were cleared up. The average was between three and four major psychosocial problems per family. One interesting thing that happened was that as families began to trust the project workers they let them know more of what really was happening in their lives. For a time it appeared that so far as official agency records were concerned, the families would end up with more problems than they had before entering the project.

As workers got a fuller picture of the families and were able to organize services, there was a change in the public welfare aura of working in constant crisis. One result stemming from this was that families stayed together. In the first year of the project no children from these families were placed in foster care.

While the families still have and continue to develop problems, the project staff is generally prepared to cope with them. The greatest limits on further improvements are due to lack of community resources. Often public welfare takes the blame for these deficiencies. For example, when the school system cannot provide a high school class for a cerebral palsied child of normal intelligence, a blighted life becomes another public welfare statistic.

One more thing remains to be said. What has made the project effective is the trust and confidence which developed between staff and families. These families did not even approach material adequacy, and their troubles have continued to occur at a great rate. Yet they can hope. The words of one mother say it much better than I can:

> The family living project has really help me and my family By getting part of my rent Back it has inable Me too Buy more for my children and myself every one in the family living project has always treated Me like I really Belongs and this is really important when you have no one I have Always Been able to talk Freely with my worker and this mean a lot to me. and I pray that the family living project will extend.[10]

These sentiments were expressed a hundred times over by the mothers, 89 percent of whom responded to a mailed questionnaire. It would be nice to stop here and let the project rest on its laurels. But the project is ending, and people who have lifted their heads a little have to contend with their feelings. One mother wrote: "If the entire Dept. of Social Services could work directly with the people as the Family living Program I feel as though the State of Maryland would have a much better Agency." [11]

More than feelings is involved. Some answers are needed too. One mother wrote:

> After people like me that try to get on there feet will stop receiving check after June that mean we will be pinch my penny again it seen that welfare will never help these clients get on there feet far enough to say *thank you* for all you have done but we don't need you anymore.[12]

We need to relate to the now welfare scene! Langston Hughes's haunting poem gives up the best possible reason for this being so:

[10] Questionnaire 1970001. [11] Questionnaire 1970010.
[12] Questionnaire 1970018.

HARLEM [13]

What happens to a dream deferred?

>Does it dry up
>like a raisin in the sun,
>Or fester like a sore—
>And then run?
>Does it stink like rotten meat?
>Or crust and sugar over—
>like a syrupy sweet?
>
>Maybe it just sags
>like a heavy load
>
>Or does it explode?

---

[13] *The Langston Hughes Reader* (New York: George Braziller, Inc., 1965), p. 123.

The Issue of Race in Casework Practice

LEON W. CHESTANG

THE CREDOS AND PRINCIPLES which form the very foundation of social work as a profession make it somewhat ironic that we explore, examine, and discourse upon this subject. A profession built upon a belief in human dignity, in human equality, and in human mutuality should be blind to the race of its practitioners and its clientele. But any further discussion along this line—except for chastisement—would be naïve. To continue it would be to deny the realities of casework practice and the realities of American society in which that practice exists.

The realities are that the society stands for human dignity while at the same time it disrespects blacks and other minorities; the society stands for human equality while it heaps injustice upon blacks and other minorities; the society stands for human mutuality while it shuns integration of all its citizens. Few individuals reared in a society such as this can escape incorporating its practices; none can escape being touched by them. Social work and social workers are no exception. Each of us—all of us—shares or is affected by American racial attitudes. To the extent that those attitudes imply a superordinate-subordinate relationship among people of different races, which is to say racist, then each of us is racist. To the extent that individual attitudes shape institutional practices, our profession and its practitioners are carriers of American racial attitudes.

The indisputable fact is that race is an issue in casework practice. It is the intervening variable no matter what the presenting problem; it is an integral part of, if not *the* problem to be worked when the race of the therapist and the client differ.

The Issue of Race in Casework Practice

THE BLACK CONDITION

One cannot discuss the topic further apart from some consideration of the history of blacks in America and at least a beginning understanding of their condition, a condition which still persists in one form or another.

Before 1966, the aspirations and goals, failures and triumphs of black Americans were defined by white America. Not only were black Americans subject to discrimination and prejudice, but the means for eradicating this condition was set down by those who were the oppressors. The degree of one's physical attractiveness, the value of one's style of life, including the food he eats, the music he dances to, the structure of his social institutions, all were subject to legitimization by the dominant white society.

The Negro was defined as a second-class citizen who could go here but not there, who could work at this but not at that, who could come and go within the gates of the ghetto but had to move with care outside of it. He was a man who had to maintain the tensions of poverty and imposed inferiority, rejected by the white world in which he had somehow to make his life; a man who had to shape himself behind the veil of invisibility and exclusion. These were the familiar facts of life. This was the "expected" and accepted condition, and each man took his part of the common ways of coping with it.

Now there is a blowing wind—pushing Negroes against the barriers that hold them in.[1]

The majority of blacks, in an effort to adapt to what was thought to be an unchangeable situation, bought the myth of white authority if not white supremacy. The result was that an oppressed people identified with the oppressor and began to attempt to become whites in black skins. They dressed the part, talked the part, sought to escape through education, and adopted a life style which was assumed to lead to acceptance of their persons.

The tragedy of this charade was not that these machinations could never achieve their goal, but that in the process of going through them, black people alienated themselves from them-

[1] Harold R. Isaacs, *The New World of Negro Americans* (New York: Viking Press, 1963), p. 59.

selves and failed to capitalize on the strengths inherent in being victims of a common condition. The tragedy of the whole affair was that the price of piecemeal "progress" was self-hate and self-destruction. Put in existentialist terms, black people stopped *being* and became pawns in the hands of master players. So that in the end, each black man who made it, who won, was constrained to ask himself: "Am I the victor or the trophy?"

But black people today have embarked upon a journey. Their purpose is to reestablish their identity, to find themselves, to recapture the beauty of their culture. Theirs is a quest for self-determination and community control—for the right to define themselves by themselves. (The charge of "separatism" is redundant in the face of the reality.) Rejection is a key component of this process. What is being rejected is a status, a former condition of passivity and dependence on others to lead their struggle. In this process, white persons as symbols or active supporters of this rejected condition will also be rejected. White persons seeking passage on this voyage by working in the black community will find it necessary to accept expressions of black rage in all of its forms, obvious and subtle, refined and crude. Many black people agree with R. D. Laing's comments on the necessity for people to turn inward to escape other forms of societal irrationality:

In this particular type of journey, the direction we have to take is *back* and *in*, because it was way back that we started to go down and out. They will say we are regressed and withdrawn and out of contact with them. True enough, we have a long, long way to go back to contact the reality we have all long lost contact with. And because they are humane, and concerned, and even love us, and are very frightened, they will try to cure us. They may succeed. But there is still hope that they will fail.[2]

The reality of the black condition compells every black man to expend the majority of his energy in the struggle to survive. In every aspect of his life, the black man wrestles daily with the choking tentacles of racism. This is true of every black child and, of equal importance, of his parents. This is true of every black man and every black woman regardless of their station in life.

[2] R. D. Laing, *The Politics of Experience* (New York: Pantheon Books, 1967), p. 117.

The Issue of Race in Casework Practice

Robert Coles, in his book *Children of Crisis,* provides some penetrating insights into the feelings and fantasies of young black children who were pioneers in school integration in the South. As early as the first year of life, black children learn that they are different—in skin color, hair texture, environment—that every aspect of their lives is a banner of shame.

Their parents, in an effort to equip them with the tools and techniques for survival in a white world, begin early the process of extinction of aggressiveness and self-assertiveness. These traits, so necessary to the nurture of creativeness and so desirable in most other children, render the black child an outcast in most public schools, and when he grows older, label him a "bad nigger."

It is the vicious cycle of racism that perpetuates the destruction of personality and self-esteem seen among black children. It begins with their parents:

. . . femininity is only imperfectly grasped by most black women. . . . since femininity in this society is defined in such terms that it is out of the reach for her. If the society says that to be attractive is to be white, she finds herself unwittingly striving to be something she cannot possibly be; and if femininity is rooted in feeling one's self eminently lovable, then a society which views her as unattractive and repellent has also denied her this fundamental wellspring of femininity.[3]

Similar sex- and role-appropriate functions are denied to black men. Power is the name of the game in American society, and power is rooted in the ability to influence and control. There has never been a black president of the United States, or General Motors, or Procter and Gamble, or the Chase Manhattan Bank. One cannot dismiss this fact with the assertion that such high offices are also out of the reach of the average white boy. The important consideration here is that for the average white boy, *the possibility exists.*

Black men are systematically excluded from the councils of power nationally and in every city, town, and village. In Chicago, for example, blacks occupy only 2.6 percent of the 10,997 top policy-making positions in all major Cook County institutions

[3] William H. Grier and Price M. Cobbs, *Black Rage* (New York: Basic Books, 1968), p. 49.

studied by the Chicago Urban League.[4] If black people as individuals have been unable to exercise power, there is little difference in their ability to influence as a group. In major cities across the nation, including Chicago, people renewal, popularly known as "urban renewal," is accomplished without the advice and consent of those currently living in the housing, and worse, with little or no consideration by the establishment of where these displaced persons will be sheltered after their homes are destroyed. Their powerlessness is further demonstrated by the fact that when new housing is erected, it is usually out of their financial reach.

These and hundreds of other examples of the impotence of black people living in a white world are observed daily by black children. In a vague yet profound way, black children learn that somehow their parents are missing something, that they lack the ability to shape and control their destiny. For most black children, the normal childhood fantasies and idealizations of parents as strong protectors and omniscient saviors are cut off all too soon. The result is that the child is unable to introject these idealizations and use them as integrated parts of his own ego so as to insure his own adequate functioning. For the black male child, this is especially devastating since the society in which he lives defines manliness as the capacity to pursue, to engage life, to attack rather than to shrink back.

In the face of these and other apparently insurmountable odds, black people have nevertheless survived. This fact should be the overriding consideration in any attempt by social workers and social agencies to understand and to work with black people. It is true that racist attitudes of white Americans toward black people have negatively influenced and tragically damaged their personality development. But survival in this society has demanded that black people develop ways to protect themselves psychologically (and physically) from total annihilation. Any social worker purporting to work with blacks should understand the effect of that fact on the psychology and behavior of his black clients.

[4] "Negroes in Policy-making Positions in Chicago: a Study in Black Powerlessness" (Chicago: Chicago Urban League, 1968; mimeographed), p. 5.

The Issue of Race in Casework Practice

SHADES OF DIFFERENCE: THERAPIST AND CLIENT

With what I hope is at least a beginning appreciation of the black condition, let us now turn to what I believe to be the central though hidden question.

When I entered the field of social work ten years ago, the question was: can a black therapist effectively treat a white client? It is noteworthy that the question was being posed by white social workers who were ostensibly concerned about whether the white client could relate to a black person in authoritative and professional roles. These white caseworkers had accurately perceived the inevitable hurdles and emotional contortions which the white client, secure in his identification with the larger society, would experience in reducing himself to accepting help from a black person.

It is significant that this question was *not* being asked by black caseworkers. On the contrary, most of us were busy ourselves with answering that question, determined that the answer would be affirmative. This raises the question: how is it that a group of social workers with equal education, trained in the same or similar schools, sharing many of the same professional values, and possessing equal levels of commitment could differ so profoundly on so basic a question? The answer lies in the fact that black social workers, living daily within the black experience, understood the nature of the question, "Can a black therapist effectively treat a white client?" They understood that the question had to do with racism, the same racism that made it difficult for them to obtain employment, find housing, secure justice, and enjoy public accommodations. Their determination to answer the question affirmatively was still another condemnation of racism.

White social workers understood the nature of the question too. But their answer was usually cloaked, not to say shrouded, in theoretical complexities and professional mumbo jumbo which served to avoid and conceal the issue of racism—their own and that of the society. Significant changes in levels of awareness by social workers of both races free us to pursue an open and, it is to be hoped, an objective discussion of this issue.

I have indicated that in my view, racism is at the core of the question of whether black therapists can effectively treat white clients. But that subject had its "fling" ten or more years ago. That issue has been settled. In an integrated society where all men are equal, any man who possesses the proper credentials and is otherwise qualified can treat any person who comes to him for help. While this fact is not recognized in practice in many social agencies, it is generally accepted in spirit as a principle. It is understandable that the general acceptance of this principle has resulted in heightened bewilderment and frustration for white practitioners when the question of whether a white therapist can effectively serve a black client is brought up. Raised at a time when black-white relations were thought by many to be at their best, the issue of the effectiveness of white therapists with black clients seems at first glance to be only a reversal of roles, with blacks becoming the racists. I would suggest, however, that such an analysis is imperceptive at best.

Let me explain. The concern ten years ago was whether a professional coming out of an oppressed, low-status background, and designated by the society as inferior, could be accepted as a helper by a client who, regardless of his socioeconomic status or intellectual capacity, was designated as superior, at least to any black. The concern in this discussion is whether black people, who as a group are rejecting all designations of their inferiority and who are becoming increasingly aware of their beauty, worth, and dignity, can be served effectively by caseworkers who symbolize the oppressor who perpetuated the very condition which they are rejecting.

These are two different kinds of questions. The first grows out of a spirit of accommodation to a destructive social system. It asks the question in order to find a means of adjustment to an unhealthy social order. The second, the subject of this discussion, when asked by blacks, derives from a determination to change the oppressive system. That it is asked at all represents the "working through" by a group of people whose awareness of their real condition is heightened. In sum, the first question tends to perpetuate racism; the second is an attempt to deal with racism. To

The Issue of Race in Casework Practice

raise the question of the effectiveness of white caseworkers with black clients as an expression of black ethnocentrism would indeed be reverse racism. But this issue is properly raised when it addresses itself to the contamination of attitudes, the narrowing blinding of perspective, and the absence of understanding of black culture so commonly observed among white caseworkers.

THE ADAPTIVE ASPECTS OF BLACK CULTURE

Andrew Billingsley, author of *Black Families in White America,* has pointed out the need for a social perspective on the black family. Any attempt at understanding the black family must be made in the context of the social milieu in which it has developed.

Viewed from the perspective of the larger white society, the *poor* black family is, in the main, in a state of disorganization. But viewed from this same perspective, this would be true of the majority of other families in our society. The majority group in America values—I think romanticizes—the two-parent family. Such families are characterized by the presence of a father who works regularly from nine to five and a mother who is a homemaker. Mother may be active in the P.T.A., her church, or a host of civic and social organizations. Weekends and vacation times are spent engaging in recreational and other activities as a family group. The family's goals are usually those of fulfilling each individual's potential and social contribution at one extreme and aspiring toward affluence and status at the other.

Obviously, this is a stereotyped and, in many instances, an inaccurate picture of the average white family. It is nevertheless the myth, the romanticized notion, the fulfillment of the American dream, the idealized image of an "adequate" family. Although it may never be fully accomplished, most white Americans incorporate at least a portion of these characteristics in their ideal family.

Social work, like the other major social institutions, has been frustrated in its efforts to mold the black family into the "accepted" image. The effort was destined to failure if for no other reason than that it is a distortion of reality. In March, 1966, there were 27 million working women out of a population of 72 million women age fourteen and over. Thirty-seven percent (9.9 million) of these workers had children under age eighteen.[5] Clearly, then, the mother in the average white family is not available to her children throughout the day. Moreover, the population of suburbia is increasing five times faster than that of the inner city, white fathers are spending more time commuting. Fathers also spend additional time away from home attending professional conferences, sales meetings, and on business trips.

It is ironic, though not surprising, that the majority of Americans demand conformity to this idealization by black families while the failure of white families to achieve it is ignored. This demand amounts to another racist barrier erected to deny black families the right to define themselves. Failure to achieve this idealization does not represent the disorganization of black families. It is instead indicative of the black family's "copability" in a hostile environment. To understand this, we must examine the social milieu and political conditions under which the black family was established in America.

During slavery, there was a systematic effort to destroy the black family. Black men were dehumanized and forced to act as "studs" while black women were forced to serve as "brood mares" not only in relationship to black men, but also to the white masters and their teen-age sons. Young black parents were separated and sold "down the river." Fathers in these instances were never to see their children again. At the master's whim, the wife of a slave could be taken from her husband's bed and carried off to the "big house" (or behind it) and used for the master's sexual gratification. These crass examples of emasculation, dehumanization, and psychological destruction were not the exception, but the rule. Refusal to accept this rule meant death—a fate which many black males accepted. Under these deplorably inhuman conditions, the black family was forced to survive, to piece together some kind of a defense against annihilation.

Following emancipation, the freed blacks remained subject to prejudice, discrimination, intimidation, and lynching. A major

---

[5] See Elizabeth Waldman, "Marital and Family Characteristics of Workers, March 1966," *Monthly Labor Review*, XC (1967), 29–36.

force in the survival of black people during the Reconstruction was the family. The black family, challenged by the impossible, carried out the *real* functions assigned to it: protection of its members, provision of basic needs, socialization of its members for survival, and perpetuation of the cultural heritage.

What is this quality possessed by black families which equips them to survive in an alien land, a hostile society, an environment where danger lurks in every corner? Call it with Lenore Bennett, "a certain dark joy"; call it with Billingsley, "an undefinable special something"; or call it *soul*. Call it what you will, but this quality, seen in greater or lesser degrees in all oppressed peoples, is synonymous with that driving force which compells the human spirit *to be*—to exist unshackled, rejecting indignities, and defining itself wherever it is found.

If one examines the black family in the context of the society in which it has developed, one must conclude that: It is adaptive for a black father to leave his family if the society denies him a job and then rules that only in his absence will his family become eligible for financial assistance. It is adaptive for a woman to assume the role of head of the home when forces outside the home rob the man of his authority. Similarly, if the woman is widowed or without her husband for other reasons, it is not only adaptive for her to assume the leadership role within her home, it is both practical and imperative. The black condition has taught those who live under it to be pragmatists.

To say, however, that black men do not play an important role in the life of the black family would be incorrect. Black men have always been crucial in the lives of black children; if not the father, then an uncle, an older brother, a male cousin, the preacher, or a teacher. To call them "male images" would be an unjust description of the love, the interested attention, the paternal relationships, and the helpful guidance provided by these individuals.

The feeling of community which exists among black people is the result of a common heritage, common suffering, and blackness. Blacks have understood this throughout the years, and they have responded as a community to their oppression. Out of this has come a social structure, a kind of family organization, a set of values—in a word, a culture. This culture is not un-American or anti-American but black. It is not superior to other cultures, but for blacks it is superior to other cultures. It is this culture which caused blacks to transcend their condition.

IMPLICATIONS FOR STAFF DEVELOPMENT

Today's staff development as it relates to the black-white crisis must place attitudinal change at the forefront of new learning. Social work personnel at all levels need the opportunity to discuss, to wrestle with, to feel the issues and questions concerning black people. It is a slow process, and repetition and regularity are the key components. A beginning point for such new learning should be recognizing, understanding, and accepting the fact that the major problem facing black people is not poverty or cultural deprivation. It is racism, pure and simple. Adequate communication about this fact must include the ability to perceive the subtle and obvious examples of racist attitudes and behavior wherever they occur. Individual efforts to change are important, but the institutionalized nature of racism must be understood and dealt with. The presence of this infectious disease in individual agencies should be identified and eradicated.

An opportunity for staff to deal with what I have called the "fallacy of attenuation" is a must today. In essence, attenuation refers to that endemic tendency of Americans to see less and less difference between anything and anything else. A society dominated by machines and mass production renders itself easy prey to attenuation. Generally speaking, one sees less and less distinction between the male and female roles today, and parents, anxious lest their preadolescent sons and daughters will not be "popular," rush them into adulthood. Hence, there is less and less difference between youths and adults. This need to attenuate is the cause of many of our skewed and vague perceptions of things as they are. It is not too surprising, then, that many whites see little difference between the condition of black people in American society and the condition of Americans in general. All Americans may be victimized by the system; but blacks are victimized for a very specific reason: the color of their skin. Most Americans hope to manipulate the system to obtain advantage; many blacks may want to change the system to obtain justice.

It should not be concluded from the foregoing that blacks do not suffer from intrapsychic problems. The ability to withstand a life of frustration and indignity is determined by the specific environment, the family experiences of the individuals, the availability to mobilize internal and external supports. Some people will inevitably fall casualty to the struggle. Social workers, however, must carefully evaluate and be able to distinguish between systemic (institutional) impediments and localized (intrapsychic) problems. "Treatment" of an unemployed father may mean helping him become involved in an action group whose objective is to open the job market by removing the irrelevant credential requirements. Treatment of those persons whose ability to cope has broken down should be provided in the context of black culture, the black condition, and the black experience. To do this requires that the caseworker's efforts proceed in a manner compatible with the client's life style, communication patterns, and individual and community values and goals. The reader should not misconstrue the above as suggesting that blacks are to be responded to in a stereotyped manner or that the same treatment approach can be used with all black families. As Bowles notes:

Such assumptions are inaccurate and misleading. Despite the similar economic, educational and social circumstances which these families share, they cannot be reduced to one type of family. There is a wide variation in child rearing practices and philosophies, physical care of children and apartments, family organization, individual functioning levels, interpersonal styles, as there is in values and goals generally.[6]

The point being made here is that the caseworker must go beyond perceiving the client's dysfunction. He must perceive the extra increment of dysfunction imposed by his blackness. He must understand, therefore, that much of the behavior viewed as dysfunctional may in fact exemplify ingenuity, creativity, and great strength. Because the caseworker is likely to be dealing with a life style whose values and objectives have been conditioned by

[6] Dorcas L. Bowles, "Casework with Disadvantaged Negro Families: Approaches, Techniques, and Theoretical Implications," Institute for Juvenile Research (Chicago), *Research Report*, Vol. V, No. 11 (1968), 4.

a culture with which he may be unfamiliar, his task is to become empathically sensitive to the client's unique cultural experience as well as knowledgeable about the culture so that the service offered can have an increased possibility for success.

Finally, it must be candidly admitted that because the majority of the problems with which we deal are symptoms of institutionalized racism, much of what we call casework with the poor are stopgap measures which are at best aids to survival and at worst, perpetuation of the problem. But because it is necessary to survive in order to hasten the systemic change needed ultimately to deal with the existing problems, caseworkers are ethically and humanly bound to equip themselves to be as masterful as possible in meeting the challenge of a twofold responsibility: assisting their clients to cope with a destructive social order and hastening a change in that social order so that both the client and the caseworker will be liberated.

Realistic Planning for the Day Care Consumer

I. ARTHUR C. EMLEN

IN THE RHETORIC used to support an increasing national enthusiasm for day care facilities and child development programs there is a strong element of disparagement of privately arranged child care.[1] The working mother's use of "unsupervised" neighborhood homes has been singled out as an especially questionable form of day care,[2] and the prevalence of these informal arrangements is presumed to offer an index of need for organized day care facilities.[3] How valid is this reasoning? How well confirmed are the assumptions involved? Does the evidence support the theory that private arrangements provide an unsatisfactory quality of care? Of more practical significance, is it reasonable to assume that the users of neighborhood day care would accept alternative forms of day care if they were available?

The facts seem to indicate that the widespread nonuse of organized facilities is rooted in understandable patterns of behavior.

[1] Examples of this attitude may be found almost daily in newspaper reports of official speeches made in behalf of day care. See also documents such as the *Federal Interagency Day Care Requirements*, approved by the U.S. Department of Health, Education, and Welfare, U.S. Office of Economic Opportunity, and U.S. Department of Labor, September 23, 1968, as well as recent material issued by the Day Care and Child Development Council of America, Inc., such as, *Voice for Children* and the *Community Coordinated Child Care (4-C) Handbook*.

[2] Milton Willner, "Day Care: a Reassessment," *Child Welfare*, XLIV (1965), 125 33; Florence A. Ruderman, *Child Care and Working Mothers: a Study of Arrangements Made for Daytime Care of Children* (New York: Child Welfare League of America, 1968), pp. 62–63.

[3] Day Care and Child Development Council of America, Inc., "Fact Sheet" (1969); Beatrice Rosenberg and Pearl G. Spindler, "Facts about Day Care," Women's Bureau, U.S. Department of Labor (Washington, D.C.: U.S. Government Printing Office, 1969); Welfare Council of Metropolitan Chicago, Division of Planning and Research, *Day Care of Children in Chicago: Needs and Resources, by Community Areas* (Publication No. 1025, 1967), p. 19.

The apparent recalcitrance of the day care consumer, when examined closely, is found to be actually a realistic choice among alternative child care arrangements. Each arrangement may be seen as a unique solution for a complicated equation of family life in which beliefs and aspirations are balanced by social experience and the force of circumstances.

Professional perspectives on day care tend to emphasize the welfare and development of the child, and this emphasis has been intensified by the burgeoning interest in child development programs. It is difficult to criticize official thinking about day care programs for being child-oriented; day care must indeed be evaluated in terms of its benefits to the child. Yet there are conditions which prevent families from taking advantage of the resources that are made available to them.

The findings of Head Start research point to the importance of parental behavior and family differences as mediators of the child's success in child development programs.[4] In his freedom to make supplemental child care arrangements of his own choosing, the day care consumer has proved remarkably resistant to the efforts of agencies to recommend their own wares. Therefore, unless the nation is going to pursue coercive policies and attempt to dictate the choice of the day care consumer, it behooves child welfare spokesmen to be less exclusively preoccupied with what they themselves think is important about child care and to pay serious attention to how day care arrangements are evaluated by the users. Realistic planning for the day care consumer calls for a pluralistic approach based on sympathetic inquiry into why people make the arrangements that they do and how they go about it.

The most salient fact about the child care arrangements of working mothers is that a wide variety of relatives and nonrelatives are being pressed into service across the country, and only a small percentage of the children are served by organized day care facilities. A 1965 national census [5] found that 72 percent of

---

[4] Edith H. Grotberg, ed., *Critical Issues in Research Related to Disadvantaged Children* (Princeton, N.J.: Educational Testing Service, 1969).

[5] Seth Low and Pearl G. Spindler, *Child Care Arrangements of Working Mothers in the United States*, Children's Bureau Publication No. 461-1968 (Washington, D.C.: U.S. Government Printing Office, 1968), p. 71.

Planning for the Day Care Consumer

the children under six years of age of full-time working mothers were cared for either at home or by kin. Eight percent were in public, voluntary, or commercial group day care facilities, while 20 percent were in out-of-home arrangements with nonrelatives. As a result of the new programs funded by federal agencies and other efforts to provide high-quality day care, new groups of children have been reached, but the fact must be faced that probably 90 percent of the children of working mothers remain untouched by organized day care programs.

Whether from preference or from necessity, when families turn outside the home and beyond kinship resources, they are most likely to make arrangements for their children in the home of a friend, neighbor, baby-sitter, or other nonrelative. Almost all of these family day care arrangements are unlicensed,[6] and they are contracted privately and informally at the neighborhood level without benefit of social agency. According to conservative official estimates, over half a million children under six are in private family day care arrangements at any given time.[7]

EVALUATING NEIGHBORHOOD FAMILY DAY CARE

How, then, should neighborhood day care be viewed? Is this a casual and inherently unstable economic and social arrangement that results in neglect and chaotic discontinuity of care for hundreds of thousands of children? Or is this a creative, emerging, cultural pattern of child care in which a familiar and nurturant neighbor provides an "extended family"—kith, though not kin—that has potential for enriching the lives of hundreds of thousands of children?

The official bias is that these arrangements are of doubtful quality, along with all child care that is not supervised by an agency or provided by a day care center. In the jargon of the child welfare field, these are "unsupervised" arrangements, and they are unacceptable for that reason. In the rhetoric of educators, social workers, and perhaps the public sector generally, these arrangements are "custodial" in nature and lack educational merit or developmental enrichment. "Mere baby-sitting" is a fre-

[6] Rosenberg and Spindler, *op. cit.*, p. 1.   [7] Low and Spindler, *op. cit.*, p. 71.

quently heard slur, and even a wholesale charge of "neglect" is made. In a recent "Fact Sheet"[8] the Day Care and Child Development Council of America lamented the situation of 10.5 million children under twelve simply because they were not in a day care center, featuring this fact under the headline, "NEGLECT." Others are apt to use the same figures as evidence of the need for day care facilities.[9]

"Neglect," "mere baby-sitting"—these terms, which stereotype the child care arrangements of a vast group of families, are used to promote a "party line" in day care programming. Perhaps the disparaging language reflects widespread anxiety about the quality of child care or uncertainty about how to evaluate it, and perhaps the concept is an effort to make a distinction between minimal custodial care and the care that nurtures, stimulates, and enriches a child's life. With astonishing lack of logic, however, the worst of private family day care is thus contrasted with the best of group care in a child development center.

Available research findings do not support any wholesale charge of neglect against private family day care. Although dramatic instances of neglect and substandard care can be cited,[10] family day care is a solution that for the majority of children involved probably creates only subtle deprivations mixed with subtle enrichments. Since most maternal employment requires the use of supplemental child care resources, one might suppose that available research on the effects of maternal employment on children

[8] Day Care and Child Development Council of America, Inc., *op. cit.*

[9] The conceptual problem of defining "need" is ignored in most accounts by simply reporting numbers of working mothers and their child care arrangements. See Mary Dublin Keyserling, *Working Mothers and the Need for Child Care Services*, Women's Bureau, U.S. Department of Labor (Washington, D.C.: U.S. Government Printing Office, 1968); Low and Spindler, *op. cit.*; Welfare Council of Metropolitan Chicago, *op. cit.* For a more careful attempt to define "need" and to compare the empirical results of using different operational definitions, see Jack Wiener, *Survey Methods for Determining the Need for Services to Children of Working Mothers*, Children's Bureau (Washington, D.C.: U.S. Government Printing Office, 1956). A definition of day care need as "normal" is given by Florence A. Ruderman, "Conceptualizing Needs for Day Care: Some Conclusions Drawn from the Child Welfare League Day Care Project," *Child Welfare*, XLIV (1965), 207–13.

[10] Willner, *op. cit.*, p. 125; Sid Ross, "Who Takes Care of Your Children?" *Parade Magazine*, March 5, 1967, pp. 18–21; Elizabeth Herzog, *Children of Working Mothers*, Children's Bureau Publication No. 382–1960 (Washington, D.C.: U.S. Government Printing Office, 1960), pp. 12–16.

would provide evidence concerning the effects of different types of day care. So far, however, the studies have failed to take into account the various types of day care arrangements, and maternal employment status per se has not been found directly associated with adverse effects on children.[11] It is important to bear in mind that many of the important factors that determine outcomes for the child arise not from the form of supplemental child care but from characteristics of the child, parental behaviors, and from conditions of family life. It is reasonable to be concerned about the effects of extreme discontinuity and insufficiency of care, and one might speculate about some of the more subtle possible effects of child rearing that is shared with a sitter, but the impact of different types of private family day care as special kinds of child-rearing environments have yet to be reported.

Although there is a lack of research that directly assesses the effects on children, some research does describe the attributes of neighborhood day care. The working mothers themselves, for example, for the most part have reported family day care to be a moderately satisfactory solution despite its inherent strains. Generally favorable global impressions of sitters by working mothers were reported by Perry [12] in a Spokane study, and the 1965 special census found only approximately 10 percent of the family day care children in at least "somewhat unsatisfactory" arrangements, according to the mothers' reports.[13] In a probability sample of urban families, however, Ruderman found that 31 percent of family day care users reported a moderate or higher level of dissatisfaction with their arrangements, and described some of the

[11] For example, the apparent association between juvenile delinquency and maternal employment is largely attributable to inadequate supervision. See Travis Hirschi and Hanan C. Selvin, *Delinquency Research: an Appraisal of Analytic Methods* (New York: Free Press, 1967), pp. 237–42. A number of reviews of this literature are available. See Herzog, *op. cit.*, pp. 16–31; Lois M. Stolz, "Effects of Maternal Employment on Children: Evidence of Research," *Child Development*, XXXVII (1960), 749–82; F. Ivan Nye and Lois Wladis Hoffman, *The Employed Mother in America* (Chicago: Rand McNally, 1963). For a broad review of deprivation research, see *Perspectives on Human Deprivation: Biological, Psychological, and Sociological* (Washington, D.C.: National Institute of Child Health and Human Development, 1968).

[12] Joseph B. Perry, "The Mother Substitutes of Employed Mothers: an Exploratory Inquiry," *Marriage and Family Living*, XXIII (1961), 362–67.

[13] Low and Spindler, *op. cit.*, pp. 25, 110.

strains involved in this form of care.[14] In a New York sample that was less representative but more intensively studied, Willner found reason to be concerned about substandard housing conditions but not about the caretakers themselves, persons whom he described generally as "qualified," "warm," and "mature, responsible women."[15]

The women who use or provide private family day care have proved to be somewhat resistant to survey research, with the result that samples are apt to be biased toward the more successful and presentable examples of family day care.[16] A research project in Portland, Oregon, known as the Field Study of the Neighborhood Family Day Care System,[17] has made an effort to study as wide a range as possible in the working mother's use of neighborhood babysitters for the child under six. The Field Study used informal social contacts at the neighborhood level to locate a sample for longitudinal studies of family day care arrangements. From this neighborhood vantage point one is impressed initially with the difficulty of making stable arrangements and the amount of turnover. In view of the instability of many arrangements, questions regarding the insufficiency of care in any given arrangement are matched in importance by those concerning discontinuity of care. There are mothers who make one unsatisfactory arrangement after another, exposing their children to chaotic, discontinuous care. On the other hand, there are mothers who have maintained the same family day care arrangements for many years.

One's perspective on the stability of family day care arrangements is determined very much by the kind of sample one is able

[14] Ruderman, *Child Care* . . . , p. 242.
[15] Milton Willner, "Unsupervised Family Day Care in New York City," *Child Welfare*, XLVIII (1969), 342–47.
[16] *Ibid.*, p. 342.
[17] This is a research project of the Tri-County Community Council and Portland State University, supported by the U.S. Department of Health, Education, and Welfare, Children's Bureau Grant #R-287. The Field Study also includes a service component called the Day Care Neighbor Service. This service, directed by Alice H. Collins, is described in Alice H. Collins, Arthur C. Emlen, and Eunice L. Watson, "The Day Care Neighbor Service: an Interventive Experiment," *Community Mental Health Journal*, V (1969), 219–24, and Alice H. Collins and Eunice L. Watson, "Exploring the Neighborhood Family Day Care System," *Social Casework*, L (1969), 527–33.

Planning for the Day Care Consumer

to observe. The Field Study has included several independent samples. Each one differs somewhat from the others in its sampling characteristics, but taken together they suggest the kind of stability that may be expected. Three hundred and sixty-seven terminated day care arrangements, known through the unofficial neighborhood network of the project's Day Care Neighbor Service, have been uniformly of short duration, with the median somewhat less than two months. A sample of 146 family day care arrangements made by working mothers for their children under six had a median duration of six months at the time of interview, and a subsequent follow-up revealed that 53 percent of these were lasting one year or longer.

It is to be expected, of course, that samples of both new and terminated arrangements will show short durations because such samples draw heavily from those whose patterns of day care are characterized by turnover. On the other hand, it is also to be expected that samples of continuing arrangements are more likely to include the stable, longer-lasting arrangements. Although it cannot be assumed that a short arrangement is necessarily a problem for the mother or bad for the child, there was sufficient evidence of difficulty both in making and maintaining family day care arrangements to warrant attention to the problem of stability. Findings from this project throw light on the sources of stability or instability for the often quite different types of family day care that may be found. The duration data point up the fact that day care outcomes are not simply characteristic of the day care resource but are dependent upon the conditions and contingencies of use.

ALTERNATIVES TO NEIGHBORHOOD FAMILY DAY CARE

It is fruitful to shift one's attention to the conditions under which programs or resources will be used by the day care consumer. Even when there is reason to be concerned at least about some proportion of the family day care arrangements that are made in the private sector of society, the question still remains as to what approaches offer some likelihood of being effective in tackling the problem. Society's answer to unsupervised arrangements has been either to attempt to set standards for the regulation of proprietary efforts through licensing programs [18] or to compete with the private, informal care resources through direct provision of day care of high quality in an agency program, either in day care centers or in supervised family day care homes.[19] Both approaches, however, have serious limitations.

Even the licensing approach has failed to make a significant impact on the users or the givers of private family day care. In Oakland, California, for example, Ruderman found only 250 agency-approved family day care homes, while several thousand women were providing family day care on an informal, unlicensed basis.[20] The probability sample of Oakland's working mothers revealed that the "informal child care industry" accounted for at least 10 percent of the women's occupations—twice the number of those who were doing domestic work. None of these operated a licensed home, however, in a state where there is a licensing law that calls for the regulation of all out-of-home child care by nonrelatives. A similar pattern was found in six urbanized areas and in one rural county surveyed in the Ruderman study. One must conclude, it seems, that the private world of family day care probably is destined to remain untouched by agency programs unless radically new ways are found to reach beyond the traditional boundaries of agency influence.

The prevailing agency approach to day care has already received extended historical [21] and sociological [22] discussion. It is small wonder that agency family day care programs have remained small in scope, considering the elaborate formal requirements of professionally supervised family day care. According to the traditional approach, family day care is presented to the com-

[18] For a discussion of approaches, issues, and further references, see Lela B. Costin, ed., *Proceedings of the Centennial Conference on the Regulation of Child-Care Facilities* (Urbana-Champaign, Ill.: University of Illinois, 1968).

[19] *Child Welfare League Standards for Day Care Service* (rev. ed.; New York: Child Welfare League of America, 1969). For an overview of agency care services see Alfred Kadushin, *Child Welfare Service* (New York: Macmillan, 1967), pp. 300–53.

[20] Ruderman, *Child Care* . . . , p. 88.

[21] Anna B. Mayer, "Day Care as a Social Instrument: a Policy Paper" (New York: Columbia University School of Social Work, 1965).

[22] Ruderman, *Child Care* . . . .

munity as a social agency service based on a diagnostic assessment of a family problem in which the agency makes a decision about whether day care is appropriate.[23] Day care, then, becomes a planned "placement" as a type of "foster care" in which the agency plays a major role in selection and supervision of the placement. This model requires the potential user of day care to telephone or present herself to a social agency and to accept its services. The agency for its part must recruit not only the user of the service but also the givers of care to become certified and supervised "foster day care mothers."

Why have agency family day care programs failed to attract the vast majority of potential users? Ruderman [24] and Mayer [25] point to the problem-oriented character of the services offered as unattractive to the general consumer. But there is another reason which is perhaps more fundamental. There is really no compelling basis for believing that the tasks of finding, selecting, and making child care arrangements can be performed better by experts than by the individual parties to an arrangement.[26] Quite the contrary, the selection process is too subjective, subtle, and complex to be replaced by the rational decision-making of another person, especially since there is no body of knowledge on which an expert can base his matchmaking decision. In view of the magnitude of unsupervised day care activity, all that a large-scale family day care service probably should expect to accomplish is indirectly to influence the natural processes by which families go about making their child care arrangements.

Perhaps the most popular official answer to unsupervised child care is the development of the group care facility—the day care center. It is widely assumed that if only there were more day care facilities, day care needs would be met. What this assumption ignores, however, are the many powerful constraints on use of the facilities.

Even where waiting lists show evidence of need, group care

[23] See *Child Welfare League Standards* . . . , pp. 18, 44–52.
[24] Ruderman, *Child Care* . . . , pp. 338–58.
[25] Mayer, *op. cit.*, pp. 75–78.
[26] See Eugene Litwak, "Towards a Balance Theory of 'Grass Roots' Community Organization" (Ann Arbor, Mich., 1967; mimeographed).

facilities have suffered from the curious symptom of underenrollment. In Oakland, 71 percent of the organized day care centers were underenrolled, but Ruderman found that "underenrollment dominates the picture everywhere."[27] Nursery schools and family day care homes also reported underenrollment.

Why is there underuse of organized facilities despite evidence of unmet need and unmet requests for care? According to Ruderman,

The answer . . . lies in a lack of congruence between existing programs and existing needs. This involves problems of location and transportation; lack of public knowledge of existing facilities; a welter of restrictions, requirements, and priorities; and frequent poor quality. But perhaps the most basic cause is the absence of a comprehensive philosophy of supplementary child care service, within which day care could be developed as a good and attractive form of supplementary child care, rather than as either a social work service to troubled families, or a commercialized form of custodial care. Day care at present is largely unrelated to the actual total needs for supplementary child care in the community.[28]

Of course, the character of organized day care may be changing. Although the quality ratings from two studies [29] of day care centers are not uniformly favorable, it is likely that significant improvements in the adequacy of group-care programs will be seen in the future, when they are coupled with more flexible and comprehensive efforts to provide day care and related services to the community. Recent studies suggest that group day care may have enrichment possibilities even for the very young child.[30] Nevertheless, even with the improvements in care made possible by the new federal programs, it is still unlikely that organized facilities will attract more than a limited proportion of day care consumers. The reasons have to do with inevitable problems of utilization.

[27] Ruderman, *Child Care* . . . , p. 95.   [28] *Ibid.*, p. 96.
[29] *Ibid.*, pp. 109–15; Elizabeth Prescott and Elizabeth Jones with Sybil Kritchevsky, *Day Care as a Child-rearing Environment: an Observational Study of Day Care Program* (Pasadena, Calif.: Pacific Oaks College, 1967).
[30] *On Rearing Infants and Young Children in Institutions*, Children's Bureau Research Reports No. 1 (Washington, D.C.: U.S. Department of Health, Education, and Welfare, 1967); Laura L. Dittman, ed., *Early Child Care: the New Perspectives* (New York: Atherton Press, 1968).

SOME DETERMINANTS OF DAY CARE USE

Why do we make such a pessimistic prediction? It is because the crucial issue is not so much whether or not the day care resource offers high quality of care but what, in addition, are the other conditions that determine the use of day care resources. In spite of sophisticated thinking about standards, the field is just beginning to do its elementary homework on the problem of utilization. Little attention has been given, for example, to the way in which day care users perceive the benefits to the child or to themselves and how these benefits balance with the realistic requirements for arrangements that are conveniently located, flexible in hours, responsive to emergencies, dependable, and reasonable in cost. Equally compelling may be the desire for arrangements that are congenial in values, socially approachable, comfortably familiar, and that have manageable contractual and personal relationships.

The utilization issue is illustrated by the experience of Operation Alphabet, a project in Philadelphia which found creative solutions to the day care problems of AFDC families: "We were assuming that AFDC mothers would welcome the opportunity to place their children in approved day care centers. As a few vacancies opened up mothers were referred to them. Most of the referrals didn't take." [31] The project became successful when it adapted flexibly to the life styles of the families themselves, accepting their expressed preference for neighbors and friends as their child care resources.[32]

It should be recognized that the factors that determine nonuse of organized facilities involve far more than the age limitations for group care or other constraints imposed by the facility itself as a matter of policy. Although utilization factors are many, complex, and interrelated, it will suffice to discuss the significance of only three: family size; distance from home to the day care resource; and stated preference for type of care.

[31] Audrey Pittman, "Operation Alphabet: the Enabler," *Public Welfare*, XXVII (1969), 23.
[32] *Ibid.*, pp. 23, 24.

Family size. Perhaps the most important constraint upon the ability of a family to use a group care facility is the number of children in the family who need this type of arrangement. But it is important to recognize that the same is true where neighborhood sitters are concerned and relatives who provide out-of-home arrangements. Ruderman found only one child per arrangement in 75 percent of day care center usage and in 70 percent of care by neighborhood sitters.[33] In screening 494 working mothers for one of the samples of the Field Study in Portland, families with two or more children in an arrangement were less likely to have made an out-of-home arrangement by a difference of 32 percent. Census data reported by Low and Spindler also show that care in own home is associated with family size.[34] This relationship probably can be explained most readily on the basis of the relative cost and inconvenience of making arrangements for out-of-home care when more than one child needs the care. Larger families also have more "built-in" child care resources at home.

Distance. How great a distance from home can a working mother conveniently have a child in day care? The Ruderman data show that a third of center users and 70 percent of family day care users are within five minutes of the day care.[35] Though a center may take pride in the distance that people will travel for the benefits of its program, Ruderman reports that distance from home is associated with dissatisfaction with the arrangement.[36]

Perhaps institutional programs assume too much willingness to do what is inconvenient or unfamiliar. Just as one might study the habitat selection of birds, one can observe how far people tend to go in making neighborhood day care arrangements. There is value simply in recognizing that although working mothers will go considerable distance for a desirable sitter, most neighborhood sitters are indeed found close to home. In 85 percent of a sample of relatively stable, current family day care arrangements, the home of the working mother was within two miles of the home of her sitter. More interesting, however, is the cumula-

[33] Ruderman, *Child Care* . . . , pp. 284, 291.
[34] Low and Spindler, *op. cit.,* pp. 19, 83.
[35] Ruderman, *Child Care* . . . , pp. 285, 291.   [36] *Ibid.,* p. 285.

Planning for the Day Care Consumer 139

tive percentage of arrangements found as the distance from home doubles: 44 percent within a quarter mile; 60 percent within a half mile; and 72 percent within one mile. Only when working mothers were traveling more than two miles to the sitter's home did they tend to agree with the statement, "My sitter lives too far away to be convenient."

The proximity of family day care arrangements represents an underestimate of the potentially available neighborhood day care resources, since a working mother may live three doors from a potential sitter without knowing it, or she may feel uncomfortable about approaching a possible sitter unless a third party acts as an intermediary. That such third parties perform a matchmaking role became a basis for the establishment of the Portland Day Care Neighbor Service.

Preferences. One of the first questions that is asked about the users of family day care is whether or not they prefer it as a form of supplemental child care. It is assumed that people would use day care centers if they were conveniently located. In the preference data reported by Ruderman, 44 percent of the whites and 82 percent of the Negroes who had made out-of-home arrangements with a neighbor, friend, or babysitter stated that they probably would use a day care center if there were such a place near by.[37] Willner's study of predominantly Puerto Rican and Negro family day care users in New York City found results similar to Ruderman's for the Negro population. Willner reported that family day care was a second choice for four fifths of the mothers interviewed, with group care as the first choice.[38]

A Portland sample of white and largely middle-class working mothers [39] showed a pattern of preferences quite different from those of the Willner sample and similar to, but more extreme than, the white sample from the Ruderman study. Seventy-two percent of the Portland women using family day care preferred

---

[37] *Ibid.*, pp. 306, 330.
[38] Willner, "Unsupervised Family Care in New York City," p. 346.
[39] Seventy-four percent of the Reiss Scale SES ratings for the occupations of the working mothers and their husbands fell between 34 and 65, mostly clerical and sales categories.

that to group care in response to the item, "I would rather have my child at the home of a sitter than at a day care center."[40]

The women of this sample were located through their places of employment. The sample represents a relatively stable group of working mothers who had succeeded in making relatively stable family day care arrangements, most of which were perceived by the mothers and sitters as satisfactory on a number of dimensions. Sixty-five percent had lived at the same address a year or more; 75 percent had been working mothers a year or more; and 66 percent had been on the same job a year or more. It should be pointed out, though, that job continuity was not matched by continuity of the child care arrangement. Of the 110 mothers who had worked a year or more, 84 percent had been obliged to find at least one additional arrangement during this time. The median number of their previous arrangements was two. Nevertheless, 53 percent of the arrangements lasted at least a year.

Although the reported data are based on family day care arrangements for children under six years of age, it is clear that only the older children in this sample would be eligible for group care facilities. Thus, one might ask whether the preference would hold true for children of group care age. It did. The preference for family day care over group care actually increased slightly for mothers with children of group care age. It seems reasonable to interpret this data as attributable to sample loss in the older group; that is, if a mother preferred group care, then she might well have placed her child in group care and would not have shown up in the sample of family day care users. This evidence is consistent with the view that, while some family day care users may be recruited to group care, there also exists a residual group of family day care users who actually prefer the kind of arrangement that they made.

[40] Most respondents at least slightly agreed with this statement, with a mean score of +1.23 and a standard deviation of 1.78 on a seven-point scale from "strongly disagree" to "strongly agree." Parallel results were obtained by asking respondents to rank six alternative types of child care arrangements presented to them on a card. This more complicated choice, which included the alternative of staying at home, also gave a relative ranking of family day care over a day care center, correlating .61 with the paired-comparison item.

Planning for the Day Care Consumer

UTILIZATION AS THE KEY TO QUALITY OF CARE

A stated preference is a comparative judgment that by itself tells us little about the strength or plasticity of the preference, nor does it tell us on what the preference is based.[41] The approach of the Field Study is to explore in considerable detail both the working mother's evaluation of her arrangement and the sitter's evaluation of the same arrangement. What are the important sources of satisfaction and dissatisfaction in the arrangement for both parties in relation to their own values and expectations? The next and more important issue then becomes one of identifying the conditions under which the working mother will make an arrangement that is satisfactory to her, to her sitter, and to the child, and that will endure if they want it to.

In view of the relatively inconsequential impact of licensing programs on family day care, it is important to face squarely the question of whether, or to what extent, society can rely upon the judgment and efforts of the privately contracting parties to the family day care arrangement. A complex set of conditions is involved in influencing their day care attitudes and behavior. Nevertheless, the evidence so far supports the conclusion that working mothers do form lively evaluative impressions of their neighborhood sitters and of the effects of the arrangement on their children.[42] However, it is also evident that some of these same mothers act contrary to their own judgment under force of economic circumstances and other pressures.

What is advocated is a shift in attitude and approach. Traditional, official models of day care planning have relied heavily on the assumption that quality of care is primarily a character-

[41] Such stated preferences are also subject to biases. Respondents may present their arrangement in a favorable light or compare it unfavorably with an imagined alternative, or they may simply try to oblige the interviewer. It is hard to know how much confidence to have in reported preferences, but they give at least some clue to attitudes.

[42] Arthur C. Emlen, Progress Report No. 4, Appendix I, July, 1969. Of special interest are the first rotated factors for the attitudes of both mothers and sitters: mother's satisfaction with sitter's concern for child and sitter's satisfaction with mother's concern for her child.

istic of the care resource—the person who gives care, the setting in which care is provided, and the program itself. The role of the day care user should be emphasized, and a model should be developed in which quality of care is seen as a product of interaction between the users and providers of child care. By identifying the determinants of use of different types of day care, one can direct one's attention along preventive lines toward the development of policies and practices that could change the rates at which working mothers make unsatisfactory arrangements.

The Field Study, for example, includes one such approach, the Day Care Neighbor Service, in which intervention is accomplished indirectly at the neighborhood level. Families are reached by providing consultation to a network of selected neighbors who in turn help potential users and givers of family day care to find each other and to make mutually satisfactory arrangements. The aim is to influence in modest ways, through the communication channels of this network, the quality and continuity of care that is offered in private day care arrangements.

Multiple approaches are needed, including the development of accessible group care facilities and child development programs that are responsive to the realistic needs of families. In addition, high priority should be given to devising attractive and economically feasible ways of cultivating the potentials of the sitter who comes into the home. In sum, we need a pluralistic approach that seeks to understand the varied needs of the day care consumer and that pursues child development objectives within a context of programs designed to strengthen the contributions of supplemental child care to family life.

II. AUDREY PITTMAN

MANY OF US IN EDUCATION, social work, and related professions have been called upon, and sometimes forced, to re-examine our traditional approaches to the delivery of services. In the Operation Alphabet program a move was made from the

Planning for the Day Care Consumer

traditional to a realistic approach in providing day care to families.

Operation Alphabet was a project conducted by the Philadelphia County Board of Assistance under Title V of the Economic Opportunities Act. The project provided a coordinated work and training program for the participants, most of whom were mothers receiving Aid to Families with Dependent Children (AFDC) payments. Each participant was provided $30 a month to supplement her AFDC grant plus transportation and an allowance to cover care for her children during her absence.

Six hundred and twenty-five persons enrolled in the project. They attended classes but did not, and could not, accept jobs until adequate plans were made for the care of their children: 215 children of preschool age; 106, three years old and over; and 109, under three—all needing care outside their homes. It was estimated that the project would eventually have a total enrollment of 1,350 persons and that between 450 and 500 children would need day care, approximately half of whom would be under three and need family day care.

The Office of Family Service was asked to develop plans for caring for the children of the mothers engaged in this program that took them out of the home during the day. The Office of Family Services is a state agency with a supervisory-regulatory function. The approval and/or licensing of independent day care homes and their supervision is, by law, the responsibility of this agency. The Office of Family Services began by exploring the traditional child care agencies. The few day care centers located in the target areas that cared for children age three and over had no vacancies. The Board of Education, which operates thirteen day care centers and prekindergarten programs, Head Start, and Get Set, could not absorb Operation Alphabet children as they had a waiting list. We explored the possibility of expanding voluntary day care centers and of convincing churches, settlements, and neighborhood centers that they should start day care programs. Through these explorations, many people learned a lot more about the need for day care, but we did not succeed in bringing many additional centers into existence.

We were assuming that AFDC mothers would welcome the opportunity to place their children in approved day care centers. As a few vacancies opened up, mothers were referred to them. Most of the referrals did not "take."

Two other types of day care were examined: bringing a caretaker into the home; and providing day care in family homes strategically located in neighborhoods where the Operation Alphabet mother lived.

When we learned that many of the families could not find caretakers to come into their homes and that many of the children who needed day care were under three years of age, the demand for family day care homes was thoroughly established. A cooperative relationship was established with the only family day care agency in Philadelphia that offered family day care to the mothers in the Operation Alphabet program. The agency was eager to reach out to these families who, up to now, had not used their day care services. Their reasons for not using the service provided a challenge and demanded a creativity and flexibility which, although traditionally attributed to voluntary social agencies, has not always been forthcoming.

Staffs of the three agencies spent many hours getting to know each other's services, delineating where each fitted into the delivery of day care to the child. We discovered that some of the most competent social workers were not conversant with day care as a social service, so interpretation started early.

We were now ready to discuss the possibilities and offer day care services to the mothers. Contrary to the usual process, these mothers were identified as needing day care for their children by their participation in the project, not by their independent decision to seek it. We were aware, therefore, that they would need interpretation and help to know about and use a day care agency.

Meetings with the mothers were conducted in the Operation Alphabet classroom. The team approach was tested. A representative of the day care agency, the assistant administrator, and I described, explained, and promoted day care under agency auspices. We explained how day care homes are selected, the state

Planning for the Day Care Consumer

regulations that are applied to the homes and centers, and how they are supervised.

The mothers listened intently, asked thought-provoking questions, and made equally thought-provoking but baffling responses. For example, they wanted to know the number of adults in attendance at the centers, what they did, how many toilets there were, something about food preparation. These responses startled us, for we knew that the current users of day care centers were not that interested in details.

In relation to family day care homes, the reaction of these mothers was loud and clear. Whoever heard of turning one's child over to a stranger? One might arrange for care with a neighbor or a friend, yes, but not a stranger selected by a stranger. Also, to these mothers, the use of agency family day care meant "placement" of their children. One mother said that she did not want her child "taken away and placed in a home" even for a short period of time. Placement of any kind by an agency aroused anxiety and the fear of permanent separation from their children. These AFDC mothers had always struggled to be with their children. In the long run, it was this characteristic in their life style that defeated our glowing plans to expand greatly the services of the family day care agency.

A few mothers learned to trust the workers and the agency, but only after many hours spent over many weeks. Each class was approached in a warm, friendly way, and the mothers were encouraged to discuss their child care problems. While there was no doubt that a relationship was established with these mothers, very few accepted the carefully planned child care arrangements that we had set up.

It became obvious that the mothers were using the information we brought to them, but not to enable them to use the agency and resources we had available, as we had intended. They were listening for ways to evaluate the caretakers they had chosen; some changed caretakers as a result of what they heard. When we were discussing the selection of family day care homes by the agency, one mother turned her back and said she was not interested, she had a good baby-sitter. I agreed that I was sure she had selected her baby-sitter with great care. I also asked if she would listen to the method we used, and I described the health assessment, security and safety requirements (such as keeping poison, medicines, and detergents out of a child's reach). She gradually turned in her seat, began to take an interest, and at the end of the class asked, "Will you go around and check my baby-sitter?"

Our dilemma now was to find a way, not to furnish, but to assure good child care for the children of these participating families. New machinery to deliver care, protection, and service to these children needed to be devised. Initially, the goal was to furnish good child care services for children; since parents were making their own day care arrangements the goal shifted. The goal or emphasis was no longer on the securing but on the assessing, and on improving day care services. Recruitment gave way to consultation, collaboration, and cooperation.

The creativity lay not in exploring further the offering of traditional day care services but in beginning with the child care arrangements already made by the mother. Our agencies learned a great deal in the group meetings with the mothers. More important, the agency was able to change, or at least to move from the tried, tested, traditional approach to respond to the "enabling agent"—the client. We see the client as the "enabler"; for the agency offered the service in the way we knew best, and it was not perceived by the clients as being realistic for them.

The majority of the mothers had found care for their children with neighbors and friends. Although they were satisfied with these arrangements, they did not object to but rather welcomed our investigation of them. A worker from the Office of Family Services was assigned to assess these arrangements, using the same state regulations, with flexibility, that apply to all day care homes licensed or approved by the Department of Public Welfare. The mothers freely gave the worker the names and addresses of their caretakers, and each one advised the caretaker that our worker would visit the home. It was important that the social worker had the permission of the mothers to visit the caretakers and that the mothers took responsibility to talk with them about our visit.

Planning for the Day Care Consumer

This minimized agency involvement or "intrusion" and gave the mother the initiating role. The agency worker also assumed accountability to the mother, sharing with her any questions she had regarding the care of the children and, in a few cases, helping her to see the need for change. How the role of consultant was accepted depended on the ability of the social worker to relate to the mother and the caretaker in a warm, informal, unthreatening way. With very few exceptions the worker was well received. She assessed the care the children were receiving, made suggestions, left informational literature that could be helpful, advised the caretaker to get a health report for herself and the children in her care, and discussed social and educational services.

As agency and social worker were able to listen to the mothers and caretakers, many changes were made. Although we referred to family day care mothers as "caretakers," the mothers continued to call them "baby-sitters." Eventually, we also referred to them as "sitters." We found that this compromise did not alter the quality of care and found the truism in the saying that a rose by any other name is just as sweet.

We also learned how agency regulations could be adjusted in order to fit the service to existing social roles and not to superimpose an agency model. Also, the worker began where the mother's and the sitter's interests were—in the here and now, in the specifics of day care arrangements rather than in the theory of child care and development. The worker's anxiety about the child's development, stimulation received, communication patterns, and so forth, had to be disciplined and approached at the right time. When a good and trusting relationship was established, the informal, relaxed talk with the sitters turned out to be childhood development sessions, with the sitters taking an active part and learning.

A further demonstration of the mothers' exercise of initiative was their assuming responsibility for financial arrangements with their sitters. Operation Alphabet was prepared to pay for the care while the mothers were enrolled. The mothers, however, made their own arrangements; a fee was agreed upon, and the mother's grant was adjusted accordingly. With few exceptions the fees were more than reasonable. We later felt that this policy was a sound and ego-building one for families; to select their own child care and to assume some financial responsibility for it added a new dimension.

The more homes we assessed, the more pleased we became. Of the 155 visited, only four were found unacceptable. In fact, most of them were better than adequate. The worker tried to encourage some of these baby-sitter mothers to become day care mothers for the day care agency. None of them was interested. They were willing to offer this service only for a friend and neighbor. They too were not interested in agency affiliation.

Several conclusions may be drawn from this experience.

The development of day services for children of AFDC mothers must "begin where the client is." It must start with the rationale that "mother knows best" and thus foster her independent rather than her dependent functioning.

Mothers' sense of responsibility for their children's welfare should be encouraged, and they should be shown that we have trust in their parental love. This premise is the reverse of the stereotype: "Because you are on public assistance, you do not know what is best for your child. Therefore while encouraging you to enroll for work or training we will select the day care for your child."

The social network of the neighborhoods where these mothers live is organized, cohesive, and often represents an extended family relationship. They are composed of individuals who become helpful and creative during times of crisis (and crises are everyday occurrences). Added to the experience of working with mothers who had strengths and abilities beyond our greatest expectations was the rewarding feeling that agencies, even a bureaucracy, can move from the traditional to a realistic approach, with the client being the enabler and forming a creative linkage to the agency.

The Bases of Social Treatment

CHARLES GARVIN and PAUL GLASSER

THE "GENERIC" VERSUS THE "SPECIFIC" has been an issue in social work since the profession began. At various periods it took different forms: policy versus practice; particularization of differences in practice by setting or "field"; characterization of differences by method (casework, group work, community organization, administration and research), and so on.[1] Once again this issue is in the forefront of current thinking, both in the agencies and in the development of curricula in schools of social work.

Since the end of the Second World War many developments have taken place in the social welfare field and in the social work profession, requiring changes in practitioner approaches. Most of these alterations have been piecemeal and relatively independent of each other. However, when they are considered together it is easier to comprehend the necessity for a shift in social work practice.

Social and behavioral sciences. The direct-practice methods, particularly social casework, went through an era in the 1930s and the 1940s when psychoanalytic theory had a dominant influence on the rationale for worker interventions. One can understand why this occurred. In a newly emerging profession the practitioner needed a theory to demonstrate his competence to himself, his colleagues, his clients, and the lay public. Freudian theory seemed to fit the requirements well. It had an aura of scientific validity, seemed applicable to a great variety of personal situations, and was increasingly used by psychiatrists. Further, the other social and behavioral sciences were underdeveloped, and their disciples showed little interest in applying what was known to human problems.

[1] Harriett M. Bartlett, *Analyzing Social Work Practice by Fields* (New York: National Association of Social Workers, 1961).

By the late 1940s, however, social workers began to realize that they had a theory without a method. Freud, who began his career as a neurologist, believed that personality developed out of the interaction of the physiological system with experiences in the first years of life. The strength of such characteristics (core or basic personality) could only be changed through psychoanalytic methods, which took many years of intensive therapy and seemed to be most widely used with, and applicable to, middle-class neurotics. It became apparent that social workers saw persons with specifiable problems who often did not fit the definition of neurotic, and they were required to help people do something about their problems in a relatively short period of time. Much professional energy went into attempting to resolve these issues.[2]

The first step taken out of this dilemma, with practitioners in other professions, was the development of ego psychology, which emphasized the individual's use of reality in the here and now. This made it possible to introduce role theory, small-group and social psychological theory more broadly defined, and finally learning theory and its application in behavior modification techniques.[3] Distinctions between one-to-one and small-group intervention processes became less clear as some of the common psychological and social psychological processes involved were noted.

New methods of practice. Simultaneously, new means to achieve client change were emerging. Some but not all of these were related to theory development. The Second World War, primarily because of the demands placed upon the therapist, led to the increasing use of small-group intervention methods and short-term crisis treatment. Among other approaches the social worker has been exposed to in recent years are marital and family therapy, guided group interaction, T-groups and sensitivity training, real-

---

[2] These issues took many forms: Who was and who had the right to practice insight therapy, and what type of training was required? How long must the practitioner with the master's degree in social work be supervised after he receives his degree? How can traditional theory be used with nonneurotic (psychotic and character) disorders? The literature of the thirties and forties is replete with articles on these subjects.

[3] Merlin Taber and Iris Shapiro, "Social Work and Its Knowledge Base: a Content Analysis of the Periodical Literature," *Social Work*, X, No. 4 (1965), 100–106; Marvin Silverman, "Knowledge in Social Group Work: a Review of the Literature," *ibid.*, XI, No. 3 (1966), 56–62.

The Bases of Social Treatment

ity therapy, group psychotherapy, group counseling, and a variety of behavior modification techniques aimed at changing the antecedent or consequent conditions of client problems.[4] This array obscures the traditional distinctions between casework and group work practice.

New types of clients. Despite the depression in the thirties and the war in the forties, professionals were predominantly oriented to private agency practice. Psychological help was more statusful than the alleviation of environmental conditions, and long-term insight therapy was the practice ideal. Unfortunately, these methods, if they worked at all, were used primarily with the middle-class.[5] But although the white-collar population grew rapidly during the forties and early fifties, the demand for services by blue-collar workers became apparent, and with the war on poverty, demands for services to the public assistance client, the migrant worker, and the inner-city black man could no longer be easily ignored.

In addition, even the middle-class client seemed different. The classical syndrome of hysteria was hardly ever seen. The more typical cases of clients with anxiety neuroses reaching out for help were becoming fewer. They were being replaced by persons who acted out against the community and its institutions (delinquents, school behavior problems, criminals) or who withdrew from

[4] Only one among many publications on each method is cited here: (*a*) marital and family therapy: Nathan W. Ackerman, "Family Therapy," in Silvano Arieti, ed., *American Handbook of Psychiatry* (New York: Basic Books, 1966), III, 201–13; (*b*) guided group interaction: Frank R. Scarpitti and Richard M. Stephenson, "The Use of the Small Group in the Rehabilitation of Delinquents," *Federal Probation*, XXX, No. 3 (1966), 45–50; (*c*) T-groups and sensitivity training: C. G. Gifford, "Sensitivity Training and Social Work," *Social Work*, XIII, No. 2 (1968), 78–86; (*d*) reality therapy: William Glasser, *Reality Therapy* (New York: Harper & Row, 1965); (*e*) group counseling: Rosemary C. Sarri and Robert D. Vinter, "Group Treatment Strategies in Juvenile Correctional Programs," *Crime and Delinquency*, XI (1965), 326–40; (*f*) group psychotherapy: Nathan Ackerman, "Psychoanalysis and Group Psychotherapy," in Max Rosenbaum and Milton Berger, eds., *Group Psychotherapy and Group Function* (New York: Basic Books, Inc., 1963), pp. 250–60; (*g*) behavior modification: Edwin J. Thomas, "Selected Sociobehavioral Techniques and Principles: an Approach to Interpersonal Helping," *Social Work*, XIII, No. 1 (1968), 12–26.

[5] These ideas are reflected in the issues briefly mentioned in footnote 2. For documentation of the class issue, see Richard A. Cloward and Irwin Epstein, "Private Social Welfare's Disengagement from the Poor: the Case of Family Adjustment Agencies," in Mayer N. Zald, ed., *Social Welfare Institutions* (New York: John Wiley & Sons, Inc., 1965), pp. 623–44.

participation in the "establishment" (alcoholics, drug addicts). Since the number of such clients seemed to be increasing so rapidly that there was little possibility that all could be treated, the profession became interested in preventive intervention at the interpersonal as well as community and societal levels. Some of the newer approaches had to be tried since the older ones were not effective, and one's specialization as a caseworker or a group worker again became more and more irrelevant.

New sources of funds. These trends were reinforced through the use of tax-supported funds for professional positions, particularly through the Department of Health, Education, and Welfare and the Office of Economic Opportunity. Some of the money went directly to established tax-supported agencies to upgrade practice and increase the number of professionals in administration, supervision, and practice. Some of the money went to the private agencies on a contractual basis, in which they agreed to provide additional or new services to low-income and other high-risk and/or deviant groups. Some of the money went to establish new agencies to serve these clients, which then attempted to employ social work professionals. Some of the money went to schools of social work to train larger numbers of professionals irrespective of method to serve these clients. Some of the money went to research efforts to evaluate old and new methods of serving this relatively different type of person.[6] The effect has been to erode earlier distinctions although they are not yet replaced by well-conceived new ones.

Group work as a habilitation method. Although social group work had been taught for some years, its full acceptance into the profession can be dated to the formation of the National Association of Social Workers in the early fifties. While it had its early growth during the settlement house movement at the turn of the century, during the thirties and forties it tended to be divorced from clients with problems, concentrating its efforts on middle-class education and socialization agencies. Partly in an attempt to

[6] An indication of this are the budget increases for the National Institute of Mental Health. Its original budget in 1948 was $4 million; in 1967 the budget request was for $303 million.

The Bases of Social Treatment

identify with the large majority of professionals (caseworkers), and partly because of a new sense of social priorities, more and more social group workers began once again to work with people who were likely to have or already had well-defined, specific, social functioning problems.[7] This trend took two forms. Some of the group-service agencies reorganized their programs to serve this type of person in addition to, or in place of, their former clients. Some of the more traditional casework agencies added group workers to their staffs.[8] For this reason the designations "casework agency" and "group service agency" have little meaning today.

Many social group workers now work with the same types of clients as do all other direct-practice personnel. The major difference in their orientation is that they see the group as a means for the diagnosis, treatment, or prevention of problems of individuals.

Social agency adaptations. The social agencies attempted to meet the new demands by testing out the newly emerging methods and techniques, and by employing workers trained in methods other than casework. In addition, the revision of agency programs and the inclusion of new agencies in the health and welfare field forced new forms of cooperation among them. Further, some of the new approaches, like family treatment, seemed to fall between the realm of competence of the caseworker and the group worker, and in many agencies, the demands of the community led caseworkers to work with groups and group workers to work with individuals. Those who had specialized in one method were exposed to the methods of others, and professionals found themselves learning from each other.

Curriculum development. If group work is seen as a method for achieving change in individuals through the use of the group for the diagnosis, treatment, and prevention of problems of its members, then the curricula in casework and group work have much overlap. For example, many although not all aspects of the

[7] Robert D. Vinter, "Group Work: Perspectives and Prospects," in *Social Work with Groups* (New York: National Association of Social Workers, 1959), pp. 128–48.

[8] Robert D. Vinter, "New Evidence for Restructuring Group Services," in *New Perspectives on Services to Groups* (New York: National Association of Social Workers, 1961), pp. 48–69.

processes of intake, diagnosis, worker-client contract, evaluation, and termination are similar. Further, the worker's efforts with individuals in the group (direct means of influence, as distinguished from his efforts to change individuals through the use of the group or indirect means of influence) and to change the client's environment outside the intervention situation have many elements in common with casework.[9] Also, the organizational settings for practice are often similar now. Just as a means for expediency and efficiency it often seemed practical to combine students in the two methods in the classroom. Further, the diversity of new helping processes and theoretical orientations did not fit neatly into the old packages taught in casework and group work as students in both programs clamored for all that was new and up-to-date.

More than ten years ago the University of Michigan School of Social Work combined beginning students in casework and group work in a small number of methods classes.[10] About five years ago the first course in individual and small-group work was integrated on an experimental basis. In the fall of 1967, under a new curriculum, a new program which seeks to integrate the two methods as well as to develop a framework of its own was initiated, while retaining the casework and group work programs as well. What follows is our attempt to put into some order these new developments in theory and practice.

A COMPREHENSIVE APPROACH TO INTERPERSONAL HELPING

Basic assumptions. The practitioner is now in a position where he can and must make knowledgeable decisions about his intervention efforts. These decisions must be based upon the requests and needs of the client and the community, not upon the one or two limited approaches practiced in the past. The helping process must fit the client rather than the client fit the method. It is our

---

[9] This framework is explicated in Robert D. Vinter, ed., *Readings in Group Work Practice* (Ann Arbor, Mich.: Campus Publishers, 1967).

[10] For an early article on the commonalities in the two methods, which grew out of classroom teaching cooperative efforts, see Mary H. Burns and Paul H. Glasser, "Similarities and Differences in Casework and Group Work Practice," *Social Service Review*, XXXVII (1963), 416–28.

The Bases of Social Treatment

professional responsibility to aid those seeking our help in the most effective and efficient manner possible.

Secondly, there seems to be more variance as to what is taught and practiced within one of the traditional methods than there is between casework and group work. This distinction, based upon the composition of the intervention situation—worker-one client versus worker-multiple clients—is only one of many that can be made, and may be of relatively minor importance when compared to others.

Finally, knowledge does not belong to any one profession or discipline. All that is known and seems useful from all of the social and behavioral sciences must be utilized in the intervention process. That is why the word "comprehensive" is used in the section. It does not seem possible to have all of this material well integrated, and there is reason to believe that closure at this point in time is too early, but it can be ordered, and practice principles developed from this.

Professional identity. If social work help is to encompass what is known from all useful sources, how is it to be distinguished from the other helping professions? The authors believe that this is a relatively unimportant question; in the long run, the lay public will make the distinction on the basis of who is helped and how effectively and efficiently. This has already begun to happen.

Increasingly, persons referred to, or who seek help from, social workers are: (1) defined as deviant; (2) nonvoluntary; and (3) those for whom the goal is behavioral and/or situational change.

Social workers are becoming caretakers of the deviant. Society's (the lay public's) increasing concern about departure from the norm in many areas of social life, and the large number of social workers compared to other helping professionals, may have led to this development. In an increasing complex world with an expanding population, it becomes very important to take care of the "misfits." As part of the more community dynamics involved, this seems to be emerging as the social worker's function. While this provides greater legitimacy for his activities, it also puts him in the vulnerable position of broker between the norm-defining institution and the person he is trying to help. We are still, however, characterizing a trend, not taking a stance on the function of the profession.

Since what brings most clients to the social agency are concerns developed in social institutions, most of them are there nonvoluntarily. The prefix "non" is purposely used rather than "in." The reason for this is that many clients seek help because of the forces of environmental pressure (the welfare clients) or of informal social pressure (the unhappy spouses who come for marital counseling). And then there are many who are given absolutely no choice (delinquents, psychotics). Few of those who get help from social workers today are there because they have psychological discomfort but no social functioning problems.

Therefore, the changes sought by and for clients are modifications in behavior and/or their social situation, not insight (understanding, emotional or intellectual) or comfort.[11] Increased insight or comfort may be a means to a change in social functioning or personal effectiveness, but need not be so. As social workers we are expected to change the behavior of the client and/or his environment so that the functioning of individuals and their institutions will be enhanced.

A few examples may be useful for clarification. The child who is disruptive in the classroom is often forced into treatment by the threat of suspension from school, and the worker's goal is to enable him to manage the class environment without getting into trouble. To do this the social worker may have to work with the child, the teacher, the parents, the school administrator, or all of them. The physically handicapped client seeks help because he and others believe that he cannot perform "normal" activities. The goal for him is to find a way to allow him to function as closely as possible to the norm of a productive member of society.

Another identifying characteristic of the profession is its ethics and values. This includes means as well as ends. Social work's

[11] The relatively small statistical relationship that exists among these three studies of psychotherapy is spelled out in Herbert C. Kelman and Morris B. Parloff, "Interrelationships among Three Criteria of Improvement in Group Therapy: Comfort, Effectiveness and Self-Awareness," *Journal of Abnormal and Social Psychology*, LIV (1957), 287–98. See also Jerome D. Frank, *Persuasion and Healing: a Comparative Study of Psychotherapy* (Baltimore: John Hopkins Press, 1961), pp. 207–14.

The Bases of Social Treatment

concern about voluntary change must be separated from the reason the person finds himself in the social worker's office. "Voluntary" in this sense refers to the involvement of the client in the helping process, part of which includes his right to an explicit understanding of the goals sought and the means used to achieve them. This has been referred to as the "contract" and permits the client to reject what is offered.[12] It grows out of not only the democratic and humanitarian base of social work but also our pragmatic knowledge of what is effective.[13] This eliminates some forms of influence, like brainwashing, although specific techniques may be useful. Our dislike for coercion, however, must be separated out from the opposite extreme of allowing the client to make choices on issues of which he has little or no knowledge, and because of his situation, about which he cannot make an objective decision. On many occasions, however, the client can learn more about his options and participate fully in making a choice.

THE INTERVENTION SEQUENCE

No matter what the methods used and the theoretical approach taken, the helping process must be dealt with in a systematic way. For this reason, a framework for worker activity continues to have much utility. In outline form [14] it may be expressed thus:

1. Study and diagnosis
    a) Preliminary diagnosis and intake
    b) Working diagnosis
    c) Intervention goals
    d) Intervention plan
    e) The helping contract

---

[12] Louise A. Frey and Marguerite Meyer, "Exploration and Working Agreement in Two Social Work Methods," in Saul Bernstein, ed., *Explorations in Group Work* (Boston: Boston University School of Social Work, 1965), pp. 1–11; Tom A. Croxton, "The Treatment Contract" (Ann Arbor, Mich.: University of Michigan School of Social Work, 1966; mimeographed).

[13] Bertram H. Raven and Jan Rietsema, "The Effects of Varied Clarity of Group Goal and Group Path upon the Individual and His Relationship to His Group," in Dorwin Cartwright and Alvin Zander, eds., *Group Dynamics, Research and Theory* (Evanston, Ill.: Row-Peterson, 1960), pp. 395–413.

[14] This is a revision of the diagram and material discussed in Sarri *et al.*, "Diagnosis in Group Work," in Vinter, ed., *op. cit.*, pp. 39–71.

2. Intervention
   a) Direct means of influence
   b) Indirect means of influence
   c) Extra-group means of influence
3. Evaluation and termination.

This outline does not imply that these diagnostic and treatment processes occur as clearly separate and definable entities in the course of treatment. It is recognized that any aspect of worker activity may have the potential of both eliciting new information and providing the occasion for client change. What is being recommended here is that the worker should be alert to his responsibility to relate change activities to an analysis of determining conditions and to plan means of assessing effectiveness as a constant corrective to ineffective or even harmful treatment.

DIAGNOSIS AND GOAL DETERMINATION

As can be seen from the above conceptualizations, this approach to social treatment, whether carried on in the context of one-to-one, group, or family, stresses the importance of goal determination.[15] This emphasis comes from two considerations, one ethical and the other empirical. The ethical component stems from a concept of the member-worker contract as including mutual agreement on the ends to be sought through treatment. The empirical element begins with the conviction that the only way in which any specific treatment plan, as well as a treatment technology, can be evaluated is by the achievement of goals. A further empirical input is the mounting volume of research which indicates the relationship of goal clarity to goal achievement.[16]

The choice of goals, as well as the selection of a treatment plan, must rest upon an adequate diagnosis. This approach requires assessment of the following elements: (1) how the client and significant others perceive the problem; (2) the conditions under which the problem occurs; (3) the consequences, immediate as

---

[15] Werner Gottlieb and Joe H. Stanley, "Mutual Goals and Goal-setting in Casework," *Social Casework*, XLVIII (1967), 471–77; Florence Hollis, *Casework: a Psychosocial Therapy* (New York: Random House, 1964), pp. 204–16; Julianna T. Schmidt, "The Use of Purpose in Casework Practice," *Social Work*, XIV, No. 1 (1969), 77–84.

[16] Raven and Rietsema, *op. cit.*

well as long-range, of the client's behavior pertaining to the problem; (4) the client's goals for change; (5) the feasible subgoals related to the ultimate goals; and (6) forces both within the client and in his environment that either facilitate or hinder treatment.

ASSESSMENT: THEORIES AND GOALS

Confronted with the wide variety of methods and techniques available to people in trouble or likely to be in trouble, how does the practitioner make initial decisions about his approach to the client? This is not an easy question to answer, but some distinctions can be made on the basis of the client's problems as he and others see it. These categories are not meant to be mutually exclusive but rather a matter of relative emphasis. Combinations of approaches are often required, but a clearer understanding of the relationship between means and ends is often useful in the achievement of goals.

1. The physical and/or social environment makes unreasonable demands upon the person and his family which he cannot fulfill, and this leads to malfunctioning. Now that we have come out of the era of attributing all problems to the intrapsychic processes of the person and are increasingly dealing with those who are defined as different because they are poor, have a different skin color than that of the majority, or a distinctive socialization history, this category takes on special significance. We are all familiar with the welfare client who must manage on a budget that the most intelligent of us would find impossible, or the child who enters a school system unable to understand its language or procedures despite his willingness to learn. In these situations the client's goals are not discrepant with those of the community or society; rather the person does not possess the means to achieve them, and/or the institutions are not geared to help him sufficiently to enable him to succeed. Under these circumstances the worker must possess a knowledge of organizational and interorganizational theory to help the institution become more responsive to the client.[17] In addition, programs of education and train-

[17] Zald, *op. cit.*

ing to teach the client to deal more adequately with the institutions may be useful.

The former involves a variety of client advocacy procedures, often with the client's help and involvement;[18] the latter requires socialization approaches, which include many aspects of preventive intervention.[19] Often the two must go together. The welfare client must petition for more money, but perhaps he must also learn to budget better. The school must change its curriculum, but the child can also be better prepared to enter school through preschool programs that involve four- and five-year-olds and their parents.

2. Interpersonal malfunctioning in one or a few areas of life and/or with one or a few persons is a second type of problem. Examples include many forms of marital difficulty or delinquent behavior. Most of the newer forms of treatment emphasize manipulating the physical or social environment or helping the client give up dysfunctional patterns of behavior for more constructive and more rewarding patterns. Some would call this a resocialization approach. Social-psychological or behavior modification approaches, separately or together, are most useful here. Family therapy, which attempts to change such characteristics of the group as its patterns (structure) of communication, power and influence, and affection, or its processes of problem-solving and conflict and its resolution are also relevant. So are some behavior modification approaches, such as trying to reduce the child's disruptive classroom behavior by altering the teacher's or peers' behavior which sets him off, or rewarding him after he has reacted.

3. Some clients evidence malperformance in many areas of social life, or withdraw from reality almost totally. These persons often require the kind of help that makes it possible for them to deal more objectively with their own thinking processes and their

---

[18] Paul Glasser *et al.*, "Group Work Intervention in the Social Environment" (Ann Arbor, Mich.: University of Michigan School of Social Work, 1968; mimeographed); *Ad Hoc* Committee on Advocacy, "The Social Worker as Advocate: Champion of Social Victims," *Social Work*, XIV, No. 2 (1969), 16–22.

[19] Glorianne Wittes and Norma Radin, "Two Approaches to Group Work with Parents in a Compensatory Preschool Program," *Social Work* (in press).

The Bases of Social Treatment

derivatives. The neurotic who constantly finds ways to fail in everything he does and the psychotic who interacts minimally with his social and physical environment are illustrations. Effective treatment may require that these people review the development of their approach to life as a means to changing it. More traditional psychoanalytic and ego-psychological methods may be useful here. Certain newer techniques which grow out of learning theory may also be of aid, such as some desensitization procedures or shaping processes. Sometimes the latter is necessary in order to make the client accessible to the former or to other specific methods.[20]

MEANS OF INFLUENCE

The conceptualization of worker treatment intervention utilized here follows the "Means of Influence" typology developed by Vinter.[21] This typology places all worker activity into three categories:

1. Direct means of influence: the worker's efforts to modify individual behavior as a consequence of worker activity within or outside the intervention system.

2. Indirect means of influence: the worker's efforts to modify client behavior as a result of a change in the structures or the processes of the client-worker or small-group system in which client and worker participate.

3. Extra-treatment means of influence: the worker's efforts to modify client behavior as a consequence of change in the social environment outside the treatment interaction.

Direct means of influence are obviously applicable to all forms of interpersonal helping. The worker's techniques which fall into this category are similar whether he is working with individual clients, families, or groups and when his intent is to use his own actions to modify or maintain client behaviors.[22] This is in con-

[20] The reader is referred to fn. 4 for reviews of most of these approaches, methods, and techniques. There is an abundant and growing literature in each area.
[21] Robert D. Vinter, "The Essential Components of Social Group Work," in Vinter, ed., *op. cit.*, pp. 8–38.
[22] For readings on this subject of direct means, see Helen Perlman, *Social Casework: a Problem-solving Process* (Chicago: University of Chicago Press, 1957), pp. 64–83, 139–65; Thomas, *op. cit.*

trast to indirect means of influence when the worker seeks to modify some conditions of the treatment situation in order to affect client behavior.

A major problem for the social treatment worker is the determination of when to utilize direct, as opposed to indirect, means. Research is necessary to answer this question, but the following series of propositions is offered in relationship to this question.

Direct means should be used when:

1. The group is not yet able or willing to assume the responsibility to help a member.

Example. This might be the case if the member were a scapegoat in the group. Group conditions might be such that any implication that members help the individual recognize and deal with his contribution to the solution would be rejected by the other members.

2. Involvement of the group will help one member but would harm other members.

Example. The group is composed of patients in a mental hospital. The member wishes to discuss a problem related to sexual behavior. The worker has reason to believe that a discussion of sexual problems at this time would cause such severe anxiety that many members would seek to avoid involvement in the group.

3. The rights of the member demand that he be helped directly since he has made a legitimate request.

Example. The member has a problem and because of legitimate concerns over confidentiality issues wishes to discuss the problem privately with the worker.

Indirect means should be used rather than direct when:

1. The group is prepared and has contracted to help the member in this manner.

Example. The member has indicated that he was seeking alternative ways of looking for employment. The other group members have said that they have similar concerns and that by helping him, they might also help themselves.

2. Present group conditions are more powerful forces for change than direct means of influence.

The Bases of Social Treatment

Example. A group of delinquent boys had begun to set rules of behavior which members were expected to obey. Previous efforts of the worker to modify the delinquent behavior of individuals had failed.

3. Indirect means will increase the potency of the group as a change mechanism through an increase in cohesiveness, mutual facilitation, or normative integration, and the criteria for use of direct means are not applicable.

Example. At the first meeting of a prison group, the members began to discuss how the group might be helpful to them in their transition to life outside. While the worker saw many areas in which he could help individuals, he recognized that the members wished to explore to the fullest extent how the group could help them before they sought out any other resources. This concept also applies to individual treatment with the worker and client viewed as a two-person group. Indirect means can then be interpreted as change in the "group's" characteristics (its role definitions, the processes employed, or the use of a "program"—play therapy, for example—as a major vehicle to enhance client change).

A difficult matter, also, is the determination as to when to utilize extra-treatment means of influence instead of, or in addition to, treatment approaches aimed at only modifying the behavior of the client.[23] Again, empirical information on treatment outcomes needs to be attained. The following set of propositions is suggested as a basis for such investigation.

Extra-treatment means lead to the achievement of treatment goals when:

1. The client's problem can be identified as reactive to some environmental condition.

2. The client's problem rests in his inability to be assertive in relationship to some deleterious social condition.

3. The client's perception is that the change ought to take place in the social situation, and the worker has no basis for contradicting this. When changes are needed in both client behavior and

[23] An approach to further definition of this subject is provided in Glasser *et al., op. cit.*

social situation and the client has set his own priorities of change in the social situation, the principle of self-determination leads to respect for the decision.

4. A set of criteria supporting the use of family treatment can be seen as applicable.

5. In a broad sense, all problems (excluding some organic conditions) have a counterpart in an institutional response. This suggests that ultimately client change will be associated with some environmental change, either as cause or effect. Institutional change prior to individual change is specifically called for when such responses serve to maintain the problem and are amenable to change.

A major need for practice conceptualizations lies in indirect means, particularly the worker's activity to maintain or modify the conditions of the treatment situation, be it individual, family, or group.

THE MODIFICATION OF CONDITIONS IN THE TREATMENT SITUATION

Major conditions which should be examined by the social treatment worker are: (1) the composition of the client-worker system; (2) the structure of the client-worker system; and (3) processes occurring in the client-worker system.

COMPOSITION OF THE CLIENT-WORKER SYSTEM

Selection of the worker. Several dimensions can be considered in selecting a worker for a client or a client system, such as a family or a group. Attributes and personal characteristics of the worker can be considered, such as race, sex, and social class background. Traits of the worker, such as communication style, assertiveness, or personality "needs" can be considered also.[24] In the latter case, the worker can seek to modify his own behavior or he can secure another worker whose characteristic behavior is different.

---

[24] A summary of data on this subject can be found in Arnold P. Goldstein, Kenneth Heller, and Leo B. Sechrest, *Psychotherapy and the Psychology of Behavior Change* (New York: John Wiley & Sons, Inc., 1966), pp. 73–145.

The Bases of Social Treatment

These possibilities can be considered and decisions can be made based on factors such as the following:

1. The likelihood that actions of the worker will function to reinforce client responses may be predicted. "Reinforcement" is here defined as any stimulus which when presented following a response leads to an increased probability that this response will recur.[25] Many variables are associated with the likability of the worker and, therefore, with the proposition that his responses will be reinforcing to clients. These include similarity in background and social class of client and worker and the frequency of interaction between them.[26]

Composing the worker-client system so that it will be conducive to attracting the client to the worker is probably essential in all helping where the worker interacts directly with the client, at least to maintain him in treatment. An exception may be made when the costs of avoiding treatment are so great that this overshadows the issue of the likability of the worker. The "liking" factor is, obviously, also important when the worker through praise, encouragement, or other verbal means seeks to maintain or increase desirable client behavior.

2. A second series of worker characteristics is a consideration when the worker wishes to utilize his own behavior as a model for client behavior.[27] It has been hypothesized, for example, that imitation of the behavior of another is most likely to occur when some of the responses already exist in the subject's repertoire, when the subject views the model as receiving reinforcement for the behavior, when the subject is rewarded for attending to the model, when the subject is lacking in self-esteem, and when the subject views himself as in some manner similar to the model. The worker in these cases can be chosen so that the modeling

---

[25] Information on the operation of reinforcement can be found in Albert Bandura, *Principles of Behavior Modification* (New York: Holt, Rinehart, and Winston, 1969), pp. 217–92.

[26] A summary of available research on this topic can be found in Albert J. Lott and Bernice E. Lott, "Group Cohesiveness as Interpersonal Attraction: a Review of Relationships with Antecedent and Consequent Variables," *Psychological Bulletin*, LXIV (1965), 259–309.

[27] A review of issues relevant to modeling can be found in Bandura, *op. cit.*, pp. 118–216.

opportunities will be based on one or more of these considerations.

In a number of situations it is desirable for the worker to offer himself as a model. These include those when the client totally lacks a given response in his repertoire, when modeling is expected to have a disinhibiting effect, and when the worker is attempting to help the client rehearse behavior appropriate to particular situations.

3. A third factor to consider in the assignment of a worker is the type of expertise possessed by the worker as related to the requirements of the treatment plan. Pertinent here are the worker's skills in individual versus family or group treatment, his skills in specific task performances essential to treatment (for example, ability to use nonverbal means of communication with deaf clients), and language skills for dealing with clients from subcultures where argot is an important treatment consideration.

4. A fourth factor includes a range of variables associated with the personality of the worker. Literature is available giving empirical information, for example, as to the relevance of the following variables:

a) Countertransference effects [28]

b) Over-all personality configurations [29]

c) Similarity of therapist personality to patient personality.[30]

Determination of the nature of the client system. The major client systems considered within the social treatment framework are:

1. The client alone
2. The client and one or more members of his family
3. A group composed of several subgroups, each subgroup composed of members of the same family
4. A group which existed "naturally" prior to treatment but one whose members are not from the same family (an exception might be siblings in the same group)

[28] See Richard L. Cutler, "Countertransference Effects in Psychotherapy," in Arnold P. Goldstein and Sanford J. Dean, eds., *The Investigation of Psychotherapy* (New York: John Wiley & Sons, Inc., 1966), pp. 263–70.

[29] Douglas M. McNair, Daniel M. Callahan, and Maurice Lorr, "Therapist 'Type' and Patient Response to Psychotherapy," *ibid.*, pp. 279–82.

[30] Robert C. Carson and Ralph W. Heine, "Similarity and Success in Therapeutic Dyads," *ibid.*, pp. 348–52.

The Bases of Social Treatment

5. A group of unrelated individuals composed by the worker.

It is beyond the scope of this discussion to consider the criteria which are believed to be useful in selecting from among these five categories. An analysis should utilize the following dimensions in order to predict the outcome of treatment under varying conditions. The worker and client can then utilize this information in selecting the desired condition:

1. The kinds of group structures which emerge under each condition
2. The theoretical framework available for analysis of practice approaches under each of these conditions: psychoanalysis or behaviorism for individual treatment; small-group theory for all groups; role theory for analysis of family groups
3. The nature of norms which exist or are likely to come into existence under each condition
4. The roles which are likely to be assumed by the worker under each condition
5. The roles which are likely to be assumed by clients under each condition
6. The possibility under each condition of affecting individuals, families, subcultures, organizations, and communities as primary or secondary targets.

These dimensions can be utilized in predicting whether indicated types of treatment might be likely to lead to the attainment of goals desired by the client and/or by the worker. For example, a change in the delinquent norms of a client under dimension no. 3 might suggest that a formed group under some circumstances would be more effective than a "natural" group. For the same reason, a group composed of subgroups of spouses might be more effective than other forms of family treatment in changing norms of family behavior.

On the other hand, disordered communications among family members under dimension no. 1 might be the occasion for family treatment. The desire of an individual to emancipate himself from his family might be best achieved in individual treatment based on dimension no. 4.

What is necessary, of course, is a multivariate typology which is empirically tested and which enables the worker and client to make decisions by giving consideration to all the relevant dimensions. Needless to say, the practice of social treatment is far from this. It may be satisfactory progress at this time to delineate the variables which should enter into such an analysis.

COMPOSITION OF THE CLIENT SYSTEM

A growing literature presents guidelines for determining the composition of treatment groups.[31] An examination of this material suggests two alternatives to the worker. He can compose groups based upon the probability that a particular treatment objective will be achieved. On the other hand, given an existing client system whose composition has been determined, a worker can predict the probability that this system will be more likely to enhance the attainment of some types of treatment objectives rather than others.

A corollary of the situation of an already composed system occurs when the worker predicts that with a particular kind of composition, one technology of treatment is more likely to be effective than another. An example can be seen in reference to group problem-solving which is enhanced when an array of alternative solutions is available. On the other hand, some behavioral approaches which utilize behavioral assignments might be easier to employ when members are similar in regard to the problems and where members might then reinforce each others' completion of assignments.

In the composition of groups, one of the major issues to be considered is the desirability for homogeneity or heterogeneity of the clients in relation to a particular variable or set of variables. Variables which are included in this set usually include one or more of the following: age, sex, presenting problem, degree of aggressiveness, level of maturity, IQ, race, social class, typical defenses, and educational level. The following issues should be considered in making decisions along this dimension:

1. The requirement that clients offer alternative models to each other related to desired behavior

[31] An excellent summary is available in Goldstein, Heller, and Sechrest, *op. cit.*, pp. 319–60.

The Bases of Social Treatment

2. The requirement that clients create more or less dissonance for each other between their behavior and attitudes and the behavior and attitudes of others
3. The likelihood that similarities among clients will lead to particular structures, such as dyads, triads, subgroups, or isolates within the client-worker system
4. The kinds of reinforcement that members are likely to offer one another
5. The information available from among the members which contributes to effective problem-solving.

Another variable is the kind of role that the client characteristically enacts in other groups in relationship to the group-maintenance and task-achievement needs of the treatment system. Inasmuch as all systems require these roles to be performed in order to continue (and since there may be valid reasons why the worker cannot or should not perform such roles), compositional requirements are relevant here. Other roles of members which might be considered necessary to systemic functions are those related to the possession of expertise, previous role fulfillment (as mother, employee), and socialization or resocialization experiences (an adolescent who has been in a training school or who has had a therapeutic group experience).

The other issue noted above related to the types of goals or technologies which can be utilized with given compositional conditions. Some goals may not be possible of attainment because too much support is available for one type of behavior or not enough for another type; other goals may not be possible because the composition is not likely to produce the kind of cohesiveness that will permit the system to exist for the necessary length of time.

Different technologies, also, require alternative kinds of composition. Insight-oriented approaches may require members who are verbal; behavioral approaches may require homogeneity of problems; the use of cognitive dissonance theory may require a degree of heterogeneity. The conclusion is that the social treatment worker with an awareness of goals attempts to select with, or on behalf of, the client the best set of conditions for maximum progress in goal attainment.

THE STRUCTURE OF THE CLIENT SYSTEM

Social-psychologists have indicated that certain regularities develop over time in the kinds of interactions which exist in interpersonal situations.[32] From the social treatment perspective, these regularities sometimes support the client and worker in attaining the goals which they have mutually agreed upon; some of these regularities hinder the attainment of desirable outcomes. The conceptual task of the social treatment worker is to learn how to employ knowledge about the nature of social structures in order to understand the sources of such problems perceived in the treatment situation as well as their solution. It is recognized here that this discussion largely makes use of small group concepts. We do not imply that this approach uses all that exists in social work practice theory. Our intent is to explore here, in some depth, *one* approach to a theoretical linkage between casework and group work.

Five structural concepts are particularly useful: communications structure;[33] sociometric structure;[34] power structure;[35] role structure;[36] and normative structure.[37]

PROBLEMS IN COMMUNICATIONS STRUCTURE

Communications structure encompasses who interacts with whom about what. This interaction may take verbal and/or nonverbal forms. Workers deal with this type of problem when they are concerned about clients who dominate discussions; individuals who withdraw from participation in discussions; individuals who

[32] Cartwright and Zander, *op. cit.*, pp. 485–502.
[33] Marvin E. Shaw, "Communication Networks," in Leonard Berkowitz, ed., *Advances in Experimental Social Psychology* (New York: Academic Press, 1964), pp. 111–49.
[34] J. L. Moreno, *Who Shall Survive?* (Washington, D.C.: Nervous and Mental Disease Publishing Co., 1934).
[35] John R. P. French, Jr., "A Formal Theory of Social Power," in Cartwright and Zander, *op. cit.*, pp. 557–68.
[36] Philip E. Slater, "Role Differentiation in Small Groups," in A. Paul Hare, Edgar F. Borgatta, and Robert F. Bales, eds., *Small Groups: Studies in Social Interaction* (rev.; New York: Alfred A. Knopf, 1965), pp. 610–27.
[37] Jay M. Jackson, "Structural Characteristics of Norms," in Bruce J. Biddle and Edwin J. Thomas, eds., *Role Theory: Concepts and Research* (New York: John Wiley & Sons, Inc., 1966), pp. 113–25.

The Bases of Social Treatment

change the content of discussions inappropriately; individuals who communicate contradictory messages; individuals whose omission from the communications networks gives rise to rumor; and individuals who control the form and content of communications as a means of achieving or maintaining power in the treatment system. It can be seen that all of these phenomena can occur in individual, family, and group treatment systems.

PROBLEMS IN SOCIOMETRIC STRUCTURE

Sociometric structure describes who accepts or rejects whom and under what circumstances. This structure can be seen as the occasion of treatment problems when some individuals reject a relationship with the worker. Within the multiple-client situations, the following are examples: members of dyads who reinforce undesirable behavior in each other; subgroups antagonistic to the purposes of the group who utilize this to antagonize other subgroups; isolates; and lack of cohesiveness in a treatment system.

PROBLEMS IN POWER STRUCTURE

Power structure describes the patterns of influence existing in interpersonal situations. French and Raven indicate that the sources of power may ensue from reward, expertise, legitimacy, coercion, or identification.[38] Problems in individual treatment involving problems in power structure include destructive influence from worker to client or client to worker, the client's lack of trust in the expertise of the worker, inappropriate use of reinforcement or punishment, and dysfunctional identifications of the client with the worker.

In the family group, for example, problems often involve the powerlessness of parental figures, or, at the other end of the continuum, overly controlling behavior on the part of parental figures. Examples in the group-treatment situation of problems related to this structure are: the domination of group processes by a deviant member of the group; deviant group members who

[38] John R. P. French and Bertram H. Raven, "The Bases of Social Power," in Cartwright and Zander, *op. cit.*, pp. 259–69.

attempt to coerce nondeviant members into deviant activity; the inability of the social treatment worker to effect appropriate control procedures in the group; the existence of powerful individuals or systems external to the group which interfere with therapeutic group processes; and a deficit of task skills present in the group.

PROBLEMS IN ROLE STRUCTURE

Role structure in interpersonal situations involves the kinds of positions which are created in such situations and the expectations for incumbents of these positions in relationship to the expectations for such incumbents held by occupants of other positions. Another issue, particularly related to the concept of leadership, is whether the interpersonal situation encompasses individuals who are equipped to occupy positions which are necessary to the maintenance of the system and the task accomplishment of the system.[39]

In dyadic treatment, heavy emphasis is placed upon system maintenance in socioemotional terms, in view of the ease with which the system may be terminated by the withdrawal of one member. This function is frequently, but not always, incumbent upon the worker. Even in the group situation, a major function of the worker is to ascertain the degree to which these functions are being fulfilled.

Other kinds of roles, by their presence or absence, are problematic in treatment situations. Roles requiring specialized knowledge must be fulfilled as well as those associated with the division of labor required for specific tasks.

PROBLEMS IN NORMATIVE STRUCTURE

Normative structure involves the types of attitudes toward desirable or undesirable behavior which are held by specified group members and the intensity with which they are held. The

[39] This issue was discussed earlier with reference to decisions to be made by the worker on group composition. Related research leadership is reported in Robert F. Bales, "Task Roles and Social Roles in Problem-solving Groups," in Eleanor E. Maccoby, Theodore M. Newcomb, and Eugene L. Hartley, eds., *Readings in Social Psychology* (3d ed.; New York: Holt, Rinehart, and Winston, 1958), pp. 427–46.

The Bases of Social Treatment

content of these norms, whether the treatment be one-to-one, family, or group, deals frequently with the same kinds of issues. Such issues are attitudes regarding deviance, the responsibilities of system members toward each other, the goals and purposes of the system, and the means which are legitimate to achieve purposes.

APPROACHES TO MODIFICATION OF TREATMENT STRUCTURES

The social treatment worker can employ any of the following action frameworks in order to deal with these structural issues.

Program. A task or a specified series of steps to complete the task can be utilized to establish a treatment system structure. This structure offers the possibility of generalization into other social contexts. For example, a game that requires leadership on the part of a participant might teach him how to occupy leadership positions in other situations. An activity which rewards a participant for communication to others might enable him to occupy other positions requiring ability to verbalize.

Behavior modification. Literature has been developing which indicates that operative conditioning procedures can be used to modify social structures.[40] Leadership behavior, communication behavior, and task performances, for example, have been modified by these procedures.

Problem-solving and logical reasoning approaches. A group can be confronted with its own structural problems and can employ cognitive procedures to change such structures either through a series of individual behavioral or attitudinal changes or through the group's rational, purposive employment of programmatic or conditioning procedures as outlined above.

Changes in composition. Structural changes are effected by the addition or subtraction of members or through a change in the size of the system in addition to the effects brought about by the particular individuals added, replaced, or removed.

[40] Albert H. Hastorf, "The Reinforcement of Individual Actions in a Group Situation," in Leonard P. Ullman and Leonard Krasner, eds., *Research in Behavior Modification: New Developments and Implications* (New York: Holt, Rinehart, and Winston, 1966), pp. 268–84.

PROCESSES OF THE CLIENT-WORKER SYSTEM

One of the most hallowed concepts in social work practice is that of "process." The use of "process" is frequently ambiguous, obscure, or even mystical. The authors either assume that the word is so commonplace that any definition would be an insult, or they deify "process" as a "force" which appears to account for all desirable outcomes. It is presumed that greater clarity of the phenomenon to which the term refers will enhance the effectiveness of the worker through his comprehension of what is occurring in the treatment situation and what the effects of his own activity are.

CONCEPTUALIZATION OF PROCESS

Intrinsic to the concept of process is change. The changes of particular interest to social workers are changes in human behavior. These changes may be analyzed in terms of the behavioral predispositions of the individual or in terms of the individual's behavior in interaction with other individuals. The behavioral predispositions of the individual are frequently analyzed through the use of constructs regarding what is presumed to occur in the psyche of the individual and are the domain of the various personality theories.

The concern here is with the sequence of behaviors of the individual in interaction with other individuals. Such sequences may occur in the matter of a few minutes as clients and workers arrive at a quick decision, as a subgroup identifies itself, or as a behavioral norm is enunciated and clarified. A sequence may also occur over several treatment sessions as purposes are clarified, membership is changed, or complex problems are solved.

TYPES OF PROCESSES

In analyzing processes, it is helpful to present a clear categorization. Based upon this, propositions about causes of particular processes can be generated, and specific social events can be described. This categorization is based upon a series of dimen-

The Bases of Social Treatment

sions utilized by Sarri and Galinsky in their work on group development.[41]

1. Processes related to changes in the social organization of the client-worker system
   a) Sociometric processes: those having to do with changes in the affectional choices of some participants for others
   b) Processes of role differentiation: those which occur as either new positions are created or new participants occupy such positions
   c) Communication processes: those having to do with changes in the patterns of who communicates with whom and about what
   d) Power processes: those related to control, reactions to deviance, and scapegoating
2. Processes related to activities and tasks
   a) Program task progression: that sequence of events set in motion in response to performance requirements of the activity and related to attaining the goals of the group
   b) Problem-solving processes: processes occurring as problems are identified and solutions attempted. A related process is that of conflict resolution.
3. Processes related to the development of group culture
   a) Changes in the structure and content of norms and values held by participants relevant to their behavior in the treatment system
   b) Changes in the goals held by clients, individually and collectively, for the treatment system.
4. Processes related to the emotional climate of the group
   a) Morale
   b) Cohesion

Some authors consider emotions as a group process. Mills, for example, includes in his concept of group emotion: (1) the needs and drives which serve in the first place as causes of group formation; (2) feelings of satisfaction or frustration resulting from actual

[41] Rosemary Sarri and Maeda Galinsky, "A Conceptual Framework for Teaching Group Development in Social Group Work," in Vinter, ed.; *op. cit.*, pp. 72–94.

group experience; (3) interpersonal attachments and animosities; and (4) feelings of attachment to, or alienation from, the group as a whole.[42]

The task of the worker, then, can be described as follows:

1. The worker, with an awareness of appropriate goals, determines which processes enhance and which hinder the attainment of goals.

2. The worker develops a series of propositions regarding forces which are maintaining or could maintain such processes.

3. Depending on the goals of the client-worker system, the worker with, or on behalf of, the clients seeks to increase the occurrence of specified processes or to decrease them.

An example is the following situation. A group of unwed mothers was formed for the purpose of discussing suitable plans for themselves for the time when they would leave the institution in which they had been living. Much to the annoyance of other members, several members changed the subject each time the issue of leaving the institution was raised. The worker saw this problem in terms of the sociometric, task, emotional, and communications processes of the group. The worker further hypothesized, based on his knowledge of the background and characteristics of the group, that several circumstances were maintaining these processes. These circumstances had to do with the desire of the disruptive girls for power, rewards they were receiving for challenging the worker's purposes for the group, and their lack of skill in participation in discussion.

This analysis led the worker to include these girls in a planning committee in the agency, thus meeting their desire for more influence as well as providing the entire group with an opportunity to listen to a tape of group discussion held in a similar group. Furthermore, the entire group agreed to be involved in a problem-solving discussion regarding what kinds of encouragement (reinforcement) the girls had been giving each other for leaving and what some of their feelings were for resistance to this issue.

We have been discussing the evolution of a social treatment

---

[42] Theodore M. Mills, *The Sociology of Small Groups* (Englewood Cliffs; N.J.: Prentice-Hall, 1967), p. 67.

approach to interpersonal helping from earlier modes and theories of social work practice and have analyzed its relevance to the current concern of the profession for the deviant, nonvoluntary, client when the goal is situational or behavioral change.

The major task remains of further development and testing of propositions related to this approach. This development of concepts and models of treatment has, we hope, set the stage for such an endeavor.

Group Field Work and Tutorial Experience

BETTY A. KIRBY

THE FIELD WORK EXPERIENCE is basic to the curriculum in schools of social work. In field work, learning and doing are one; it is frequently referred to as total learning, and the outcome as "knowing it in your bones." The University of Denver, which has traditionally offered tutorial field work, has recently begun to utilize the field-center concept for the first year students. An experimental project was designed, using this method, funded partially from the Family Welfare Section of the National Institute of Mental Health. It began in the academic year 1967–68 and lasted through the academic year 1969–70. At the present time, the teaching center concept is followed in the first year, and the tutorial experience comes in the second year. It is known as the Denver Plan.

THE FIRST YEAR

One of the advantages of the field work unit that was made manifest early in the year was the support that the group offered. Each student felt quite anxious at the beginning of that first year about his ability to do the work required. As our group "jelled," it did several things. First, it helped us feel that we were not alone in feeling overwhelmed. We not only consoled each other during our field work, but became a closely knit group which met between classes to bemoan our fate. A complaint from one member of the group was taken up by everyone. Not only were our feelings of inadequacy allayed, but we gained a sense of belonging, which freed us to do our best work. That anxiety and ritual go together has been demonstrated by Malinowski, who noted how it gave groups the confidence and determination they needed to carry on productive work.

Identification with the profession, one of the goals of field work, was achieved in a unique way in the group units. Testing opinions within the group represented an important area of growth as a professional. As the year progressed we became more comfortable with our own points of view. We also came to see ourselves as others in the profession saw us. The following conversation was overheard one day after a family interview conducted by two students:

"Frances, I had no idea that you made a practice of whistling in interviews."

"Oh, that . . . well, I only whistle when I need too . . . well, you must admit that it worked."

"That's true—it certainly restored some order to the situation. Anyway, I like to see you others in action."

"I do too . . . but, just for safety's sake, let's not include that in our recording, ok?"

The unit experience accelerated certain types of learning. The first year was supposed to give the student a wide experience, thus laying the foundation for professional practice. To accomplish this, we gained experience in all three methods. For our individual cases, our instructor deliberately chose a wide variety of problems. Comparing notes on our clients gave us a tremendous vicarious learning experience. The experience with groups was much the same, with the added advantage of being able to observe our own group in action. The community organization sequence was particularly meaningful, since in addition to the exploration and assessment we did in the day care project, we also attempted to simulate the organizational process necessary for implementation. It was frustrating but well worth the effort. We soon knew what an agonizing process it really is to bring about change in a community.

Other learning experiences were unique to a group, but not related to a specific method. Exploring our feelings toward each other—we were mixed racially, religiously, and geographically—helped us grow in our ability to understand and empathize with our clients. Theoretical knowledge was gained from special projects and classroom-related discussions. Research on topics of special interest was shared. We were thus able to solidify our knowledge in a variety of areas.

A primary disadvantage to the field work unit experience was apparent in relation to the breadth that was a goal of the first year. Although our base of knowledge grew, our skills as social workers did not grow at a corresponding rate. This was due in large part to the fact that the field work instructor's time was divided among ten students. Another factor was that by plan, regular individual conferences were held at the beginning of the year, then with decreasing frequency until the last quarter, when they were held on an "as needed" basis. At the beginning of the second year many of us found that the level of performance and knowledge expected by our field work agencies exceeded the level we had reached by the end of the first year. Another disadvantage lay in the area of group pressure. While the diluted relationship with the instructor might well encourage initiative and independence, group pressure can bring about a distortion of perception, judgment, and action. Distortion was less obvious by the end of the year when the group was no longer needed so much by the individuals. Even at that point, however, the less mature students tended to rely a great deal on group opinions, right or wrong.

THE SECOND YEAR

The emphasis in the second year was upon depth, and a primary advantage was a growth in skills and in the ability to express and utilize one's theoretical knowledge as a result of the intense relationship with a supervisor. Theoretical knowledge was solidified in the weekly hour-and-a-half conferences. For the first time, it was impossible to hide within the group. One of my first recollections of discomfiture was of an occasion when my supervisor pointed out that I had missed a diagnosis to which all symptoms clearly pointed. I found myself unable to discuss the possible diagnosis with much expertise, even though I had just written a paper on the subject. I learned a good lesson, however, and began rehearsing answers to questions that might be asked. Slowly, but surely, the theory that had been demonstrated so well in class was transformed into a working knowledge that could be shared with fellow workers, my supervisor, and, most important, put into use to help my clients. In a tutorial situation, there was no escaping the fact that this had to be done.

Another advantage was that one's skills and techniques were examined in detail. Being expected to account for my rationale for doing each thing in light of the dynamics of each case was not a new experience, but it was more thorough in the second year. Although altering the recording was still a good means of glossing over mistakes, there was less chance that serious flaws could be passed over.

Observing the supervisor in practice provided further growth as well as identification with the profession. The close relationship with the supervisor, who also carried a caseload, meant that the student had an opportunity to learn how an experienced worker handled his own cases.

Further advantages of the tutorial experience related to the close relationship it was possible to have with other agency staff members, as there were fewer students in the agency. Learning is enhanced by extending the sources and opportunities for learning beyond the field instructor and the student's peers. The contact with agency staff in addition to the instructor made identification of a professional model a more mature and selective judgment.

A perceptive and frequently quoted criticism of a tutorial situation is the fact that often a dependent relationship results which can inhibit the student's decision-making capacity and initiative. Surely, however, a field work instructor should be as responsible for helping develop these capacities in a student as a social worker is with a client. As a matter of fact, it was precisely at the point where I became most dependent upon conferences that my supervisor began tapering them off, forcing me to make more decisions independently. Detailed conferences were held as needed, and this was appropriate.

Another disadvantage of the second year may be the lack of support of fellow students. The anxiety level of students is not likely to be so high during the second year, due to a more mature self-concept. Nevertheless, the anxiety that did exist was reduced by having a few other students placed in the same agency.

The outstanding problem in the current system is the gap between what was learned during the first year and what was expected in the second. It is suggested that at the beginning of the first year, when anxiety is highest, conferences be held "as needed" and more learning take place as a group; later, as students are increasingly able to accept criticism and have a growing desire to plan for the future, individual conferences could be scheduled more regularly. Thus each student might receive assistance in perfecting his work in a way that would be useful in the area in which he intended to specialize.

I feel that both group learning and individual learning are valuable. The fact remains, however, that some students learn better in one type of situation than in another. More flexibility might be built into the first year. Further exploration might be done regarding the possibility of letting students participate in deciding what type of learning experience is best for them, in both the first and the second year of the curriculum.

Preventive Intervention with Low-Income Families through the School

NORMA RADIN

It is almost a cliché in 1970 to state that the public school system is failing to develop the potential of low-income youngsters, and that massive changes are needed in the structure of the educational system if the problem is to be solved. There can be little disagreement with these statements. However, it is also important to acknowledge the fact that the child who enters a kindergarten class is not a lump of dough waiting to be molded by the educational system. He walks in the door with definite personality predispositions, attitudes, skills, and abilities which affect his response to any educational program, including the most creative, and there can be no denying the fact that a major influence on the development of these attributes is the behavior of the child's caretakers. My own study [1] of low-income preschool children, for example, shows that a significant correlation exists between observed maternal child-rearing practices and a youngster's intellectual growth in a stimulating preschool program, even with his I.Q. on entrance to the program controlled.

It follows that if educational programs are to maximize the development of the student, the school must be ready for the child and the child must be ready for school. The youngsters who are eager to explore their environment, who can communicate their thoughts and feelings, and who experience pleasure from

[1] Norma Radin, "Child-rearing Antecedents of Cognitive Development in Lower-Class Preschool Children" (unpublished doctoral dissertation, University of Michigan, 1969).

completing a task to their own satisfaction, are ripe for learning. Unfortunately, a good number of children do not start kindergarten this way, and a large percentage of these youngsters come from low-income families.

Many child development authorities, such as Bronfenbrenner,[2] believe that intensive work with lower-class parents is essential if compensatory programs are to be effective. Recent research studies tend to corroborate this view. One study in Tennessee, for example,[3] found that teaching mothers how to stimulate the development of their four-year-olds had beneficial effects not only on these children, but on their younger siblings as well. A control group of four-year-olds enrolled in a preschool class without parental involvement showed no sibling effect. Another investigation, by Karnes,[4] found that training low-income mothers to stimulate the intellectual development of their preschoolers produced significant cognitive growth in the youngsters. In a post-kindergarten study of my own,[5] it was found that significantly greater I.Q. gains were attained by children whose mothers were involved in an intensive educational program during both preschool and kindergarten years than were attained by children whose mothers were involved for only one year or not at all.

It is abundantly clear, as researchers and practitioners well know, that lower-class parents want their children to succeed in school. Study after study has indicated that these mothers and fathers have great hope for their preschoolers and perceive the school system as the major ladder of their upward mobility. The problem is not one of values that are discrepant with those of the larger society but rather one of methodology. For the most part, these parents do not know how to attain the goals they hold for their youngsters. For example, they do not see the relationship

[2] Urie Brofenbrenner, "Motivational and Social Components in Compensatory Educational Programs," in Edith Grotberg, ed., *Critical Issues in Research Related to Disadvantaged Children* (Princeton, N.J.: Educational Testing Service, 1969), pp. 1-34.

[3] Barbara Gilmer, untitled paper described in *Darcee Newsletter*, George Peabody College for Teachers, February, 1969.

[4] M. Karnes *et al.*, "An Approach for Working with Mothers of Disadvantaged Preschool Children," Merrill-Palmer Quarterly, XIII (1967), 174-83.

[5] Norma Radin, "The Impact of a Kindergarten Home Counseling Program," *Exceptional Children*, XXXVI (1969), 251-56.

between reading to a child when he is four years of age and the child's ability to read when he is ten. They do not connect an emphasis on obeying orders at four and a half with lack of inner control at eleven. Thus, helping parents to nurture child behaviors and abilities which are congruent with competence in school is merely providing them with skills and knowledge to reach their own goals. The evidence is overwhelming that these mothers and fathers welcome such efforts.

It is not suggested here that lower-class parents do not love their children or that their style of life should be changed. It is merely being affirmed that certain child-bearing practices have been shown in innumerable studies to be more conducive to intellectual growth than others, and since parents are desirous of having their children succeed in school, parent-education programs should be offered that will facilitate that success. It is also likely that participation in such programs will improve the parents' ability to achieve the changes they desire in the educational system. With an understanding of the learning process and of the school's role in the process, parents are in a much stronger position to work for changes that will be most meaningful to their children.

The major questions concerning educational programs with low-income parents and intervention programs designed to prevent school failure are: Who shall conduct these programs? What should be the nature of these programs?

It is the position of the writer that the ideal person to develop and coordinate parent-education programs is the school social worker. Classroom teachers, for the most part, are not trained to work with adults nor do they feel comfortable interacting with them. The graduates of our teacher-training programs appear only too eager to allow social workers to "take care of the parents" while they center their attention on the children. Social workers employed by therapeutic agencies are also typically unprepared for early intervention work because the focus of these programs is on education, not treatment, of both parents and children. Improved family functioning may be a fringe benefit; it is not the prime objective. In addition, discussions of the precursors of number concept or linguistic ability are relatively alien to psychiatrists and psychotherapists.

Another factor to be considered is that school systems touch and serve all youngsters. There is no derogatory connotation or label attached to involvement with an educational institution. In a few places, a local school may be so detested in the community that any program associated with it is contaminated by its very name. These situations are rather rare, however.

These factors do not suggest that welfare agencies, guidance clinics, family agencies, and so forth should not establish education programs for parents of young children as they wish. It is suggested, however, that parent-education work with low-income families should be perceived as an essential component of school social work. The inclusion is most appropriate since the goal of school social work is to facilitate the development of all youngsters in a school system, or as Alfred Kahn phrases it, "to do all those things within the school system that will help the child function as a student." [6]

The major obstacle to incorporating parent education into school social work does not lie with the parents, as we have noted, or with the administrators. It has been the experience of workers in this field that directors of special services, principals, and superintendents welcome the problem-prevention approach. Rather, the difficulty is typically found within the school social worker himself. His orientation tends to be that of a therapist who treats a patient with a diagnosed illness, instead of an educator who assists a competent adult to acquire new skills and knowledge. The difference may appear trivial, but in practice it is significant. For example, the therapist waits for the patient to come for help about his problem, or he accepts referrals from others who recognize a problem and wish to have it explored and treated. The parent educator in a preventive intervention program identifies a high risk population based primarily on demographic data, and then makes an all-out effort to reach all the parents who fall within its boundaries, not merely those who are in need of help. If the

[6] Alfred J. Kahn, "Schools: Social Change and Social Welfare," National Conference on School Social Work, 1969.

Preventive Intervention through the School

net that is tossed out brings in a few individuals who appear to know as much about the topics to be discussed as the parent educator, so be it. They are welcome to participate in the program if they choose and if they can make a genuine contribution to the other participants who are not so knowledgeable. It is usually an asset to have such individuals in the program.

Another difference is that therapists seek to have their patients recognize and articulate their problems. The focus is on their weakness. The parent educator, on the other hand, can state quite honestly that no one was ever taught how to raise children and that efforts to gain knowledge in this area are a sign of maturity. Thus, the emphasis is on the strengths of the participants. No defenses are aroused; no evasive tactics are evoked. Further, with an educational stance the relationship between student and teacher can easily be reversed when the content shifts. The social worker who is functioning as a parent educator has much to learn about children and adults who have had life experiences different from his own. He can openly indicate that he has much to learn from the parents, and an equalitarian relationship is therefore possible. Such role reversal is virtually impossible in a therapeutic relationship where a status hierarchy is difficult to avoid. That may be one of the reasons psychotherapy has been so unsuccessful with lower-class clients.

In sum, to function effectively as a parent educator, the school social worker must switch orientations and relate in a different way to the people with whom he is working. Those who are unable to change perspectives should probably not attempt to conduct preventive intervention programs.

A lesser obstacle to incorporating preventive intervention into school social work is the limited knowledge that many practitioners possess about early childhood and cognitive development. These deficiencies can be corrected, however, by reading, taking appropriate courses, or consulting with those who are more knowledgeable.

It is not expected that social workers will develop their own curriculum in preventive intervention. Much has already been written by those involved in such programs, in the realm of school-relevant child management techniques as well as of intellectual stimulation. There is still much room for more creative ideas and for improvements in the literature, but one need not start from scratch. One request for parent-education material put the issue very succinctly: the writer asked for material so that she would not have to "invent the wheel all over again."

Several models of preventive intervention programs have developed to date, varying on three dimensions: age of the child; content of program; and methodology.

Age of the child. Almost all programs involve children below the first grade. Although the programs can be extended upward, the likelihood of their being effective diminishes as the child gets older. It might be wiser to work with peer groups rather than with parents when the latency age is reached. By the time a child is in the fourth grade, his academic failures and behavior problems are usually manifold. His mother's high expectations for him have virtually vanished, and his peers have become the major influence in his life. He is lost to the streets. The youngest age at which a preventive intervention program should be initiated is an open question. Some experimental programs now involve mothers of infants just a few weeks old but the efficiency of such programs is yet to be demonstrated. Even if such programs eventually prove worthwhile, it is likely that a health agency, or possibly a new child development agency, would be given the responsibility for operating them. Children between the ages of three and seven appear to be the most appropriate targets of preventive intervention programs conducted by school systems.

Programs have been developed for the parents of preschoolers and kindergarten youngsters. Some of the former have been an adjunct to a preschool class; others have served as the entire preschool program. In one model, months of intensive work with the parents served as a prelude to a child's attendance at a preschool class. At the kindergarten level, a parent program has sometimes served to support the regular classroom curriculum. In other instances, it provided an opportunity for introducing new curriculum ideas without waiting for kindergarten teachers to use an innovative program. Although it is desirable to coordinate a parent program as closely as possible with a class program, it is not always possible. Some kindergarten and preschool teachers are unable to articulate their curriculum and/or are uncomfortable when pressed for information about their instructional program. Other teachers are rather hostile to parents, blaming them for the difficulties of the children. In these cases, the parent program may have to function relatively independent of the class program. This is unfortunate but unavoidable. Often, however, teachers become fascinated by the feedback they are given about the responses of the parents, and eventually they become involved in the program.

Program content. Two areas have been delineated in the content of parent-education programs: child management and intellectual stimulation. The two are interrelated, but the emphasis can differ. For example, in discussing ways in which a mother can encourage her child to classify objects in the kitchen, the mother is urged to praise her child when he answers correctly or gives approximately correct answers. The importance of a noncritical attitude when the child makes a mistake is stressed, for learning cannot take place when the child is fearful or the parent punitive in her efforts to teach. On the other hand, the parent educator focusing on child management strategies might discuss becoming observant of cues indicating that a behavior problem is brewing. The importance of offering diversionary activities is then emphasized, such as suggesting that the child help his mother cut out cookies. The learning that is provided by these distractions is then pointed out; for example, an understanding of shapes is gained.

The goals of the two areas differ. When intellectual growth is emphasized, the object is for mothers to include stimulating activities in their everyday lives. Asking children to help sort the washing by separating dark and light items is typical of the activities suggested. The importance of providing models for children is also emphasized. It is desirable not only to read to preschool children but also to have material about the home which the adults enjoy reading. Identification is a powerful force in the lives of preschool children and should not be overlooked.

In the child-management area, the objective is for children to develop internal control so that their behavior will not be regulated by external reinforcers and punishers. (Inner control is emphasized because self-direction is essential for success in any educational setting.) To attain that goal, reinforcement principles are introduced along with explanations of the antecedents of self-reinforcement and the effects of various reinforcement schedules. Attempts are not made to end the use of punishment so prevalent in lower-class homes; rather, mothers are encouraged to increase their repertoire of control techniques. Through reinforcing mutually contradictory activities, for example, parents learn that they can reduce the frequency of undesirable behavior without resorting to threats or whippings. It appears to be unwise to take away the one control technique with which the parents are familiar, punishment, before skill has been acquired in using other strategies.

Although child-management and cognitive stimulation have been analyzed as separate entities, some activities clearly fall into both areas simultaneously. For example, giving children choices with the proviso that they accept the predictable consequences strengthens temporal relationships and also fosters the anticipation of the consequences of behavior. The mere act of discussing choices with children involves them in decision-making. This gives youngsters experience in problem-solving while enhancing the perception that they are valued as thinking human beings by their parents.

Methodology. Regarding methodology, the third variable, two approaches have been used in preventive intervention programs thus far: one-to-one relationships and small-group discussions. The former is time-consuming but has the advantage of individualizing instruction and making minimal demands upon the parent; the latter benefits from peer pressure to conform to group norms, internalization of group goals, and use of the group as a basis for social comparison, but it is dependent upon attendance at meetings to have an effect. Thus, there are costs and benefits attached to each method.

In the one-to-one approach, the parent is visited weekly or biweekly and is given a demonstration of an activity that will be

Preventive Intervention through the School 191

stimulating and which she can easily undertake with her child. The activity typically involves use of material readily available in the home, such as dishes, hair curlers, toilet paper. At times, inexpensive materials, such as old magazines, may be left with the parent for use during the week. Often the parent is given assignments to be completed prior to the next session.

In the small-group approach, between five and fifteen mothers are invited to weekly meetings in a home or school building. Wherever possible, baby-sitting, transportation, and refreshments are provided to combat attendance problems. Discussions and/or activities are programmed for each session. In a recent research study,[7] it was learned that while discussions are highly effective in fostering group cohesion and adherence to new norms, the power of the group is exerted only on members who attend regularly. Those who do not feel that they are a part of the group are relatively unaffected. A preplanned activity program affects even the casual attender, but passivity and relative detachment from other members seem to develop if attendance is sporadic. The ideal arrangement may consist of a sequence of group meetings which start with planned activities and then shift at an early point to group discussions, with increasing responsibility given to the members for the meetings.

To illustrate the variation that is possible under the rubric of preventive intervention, several examples will be cited of programs conducted within the past few years in the metropolitan Detroit area. Similar programs are in operation in many parts of this country, and even in Israel.

In the Early Education Program of Ypsilanti, Michigan, four-year-old children attend a preschool class one half day and receive biweekly home visits when a tutorial program is conducted. In addition, weekly group meetings are held for the mothers, touching upon both child management strategies and activities which are stimulating to the child's mental growth. The group meetings are conducted by a social worker. An unexpected but rewarding outcome of the group meetings in the 1967–68 school

[7] Glorianne Wittes and Norma Radin, "Two Approaches to Parent Work in a Compensatory Preschool Program," National Conference on Family Relations, 1969.

year was the development of a social action orientation. The mothers banded together and successfully pressed the school authorities to provide an enriched kindergarten program for their youngsters. The new sense of competence which had developed in child rearing apparently diffused to other areas of the mothers' lives, including that of their relationship with the school. It was also found that the mothers, black and white, who participated in the parent program developed strong attachments for one another in spite of an initial estrangement. The improvement of race relations was not a conscious objective of the program, but a shared interest in the development of their children and in the parent program evoked empathy for one another which overcame discomfort among the women.

In Monroe, Michigan, students from the University of Michigan School of Social Work are supervised by a school social worker in a preventive intervention program of the one-to-one variety. The students work with a limited number of low-income mothers whose children will enter kindergarten the following year. There is no preschool class for the children. The mothers were selected from a list of families suggested by school personnel since demographic data with which to select mothers were not available. An interesting aspect of this program has been the effect of the feedback provided by students to the principals and teachers who make the referrals. These families had been considered as "hopeless," "unreachable." The reports that the mothers welcomed the parent educators and were making genuine efforts to work with their children have drastically changed that image. If there is any validity to Rosenthal's findings about teacher expectations,[8] these changed perceptions may have a significant impact upon the school career of the youngsters.

In the inner city in Detroit, a student from the same school of social work has been meeting since the fall of 1969 with the mothers of youngsters in a kindergarten class. The mothers brought their children to one meeting and practiced reading to

[8] R. Rosenthal and L. Jacobson, "Self-fulfilling Prophecies in the Classroom: Teachers' Expectation as Unintended Determinants of Pupils' Intellectual Competence," American Psychological Association, 1967.

Preventive Intervention through the School 193

them in various corners of the home in which the meeting was held. The women compared notes afterward about how their youngsters responded and suggested methods to one another for improving their skills. A unique aspect of this project has been combining mothers and children into one group. The youngsters became a part of the instructional program. This arrangement reduces the need for sitters and offers an ideal opportunity for mothers to practice new skills. It also offers the worker an opportunity to evaluate the progress of the mothers as they interact with their children. Thus, the approach has much merit, provided the worker has the stamina to conduct a meeting with five or six preschoolers and as many adults.

Another program, in Ypsilanti, involved an intervention program in which biweekly home visits were made to all the mothers of the children in two low-income kindergarten classes. Suggestions were made to the parents about things they could do in the home to support and extend the classroom curriculum. The curriculum director who was developing the class program helped plan the content of the home visits. The principal was particularly interested in establishing an open communication system with the residents of the neighborhood. He found the workers excellent channels of communication. They knew the mothers well and were able to transmit their views concerning the school and the innovative programs recently introduced. The great potential of preventive intervention programs for communicating information *from* low-income families *to* the school was clearly demonstrated in this project.

In Plymouth, Michigan, an attempt is being made to reach lower-class fathers, the greatly neglected factor in compensatory programs, and involve them in the school. It is hoped that the fathers will thereby interact more frequently and effectively with their young sons. A more immediate goal is to masculinize the atmosphere of the entire school. A male social worker-student, working closely with a male elementary school counselor, is making an appeal to the fathers through their masculine interests. The fathers are being asked to construct equipment for the kindergarten class and to tell the youngsters what they do at work.

Trips are also planned to their places of employment so that the boys and the men in the community will become better acquainted. The rationale for this approach is that lower-class men perceive child rearing as women's work and are not responsive to parent education programs. It was therefore decided to try to reach men with a program that does arouse their interests, tasks performed by males in society. It is hoped that discussions about child-rearing techniques and the importance of fathers in the child's development will take place informally as the program evolves.

The discussion thus far has focused on preparing the young child for success in school so that failure can be prevented. The same frame of reference of preventive intervention can be applied to other aspects of school social work. There are other roles which the students are certain to play for which they are unprepared. Working with junior high school students is one example. Just as the school social worker intervened before problems were manifested with preschoolers, he can develop an intervention program before difficulties arise which will help socialize youngsters for new positions they will fill at the secondary level. Again, the strategy would be to select a high-risk population likely to encounter difficulties, and then make an all out effort to reach all members of the group with an educational program. It is usually easy to select a sixth-grade class whose predecessors presented severe academic and/or behavioral problems at junior high school. A program of skill training and knowledge dissemination could then be developed which will include taking the sixth-grade youngsters for many visits to the junior high school, and arranging a meeting with the teaching and auxiliary staff with whom they will interact. A special summer or week-end program might be instituted in which the youngsters and some of their future teachers participate in an unstructured day camp program. This might provide an opportunity to learn about one another in a nonacademic setting prior to encounters in the classroom. It might also be possible to team up the sixth-graders with "buddies" in the eighth grade who will serve as socializers before entry into junior high school as well as during the entire first year. The sixth-graders might go through several school days with their "buddies" in order to become familiar with the junior high school routine, the location of lockers, the sports program, and so on. In this way a model would be provided to ease the transition from one position to another. Serving as mentors might also be beneficial to the older children, as many cross-age programs have demonstrated.

In a similar vein, efforts might be extended to prepare high school seniors likely to experience difficulty for their future roles as employees. A variety of employers could be invited to meet with the students concerning expectations they have for their employees. Time might be allocated for the students to visit various offices and businesses to gain firsthand knowledge of working conditions. Discussions with employees at these sites, particularly those recently in high school, would also be helpful in preparing the students for the role they will play in the near future. Where possible, part-time jobs should be arranged to give the students a more concrete experience, a role-playing experience, under supervision.

Other opportunities will be apparent if school social workers begin to look upon themselves as facilitators in the socialization process. Programs can be developed to prepare students for the role of parent role or spouse, for example. The prime questions are: "What roles will the students be playing next year? Are they prepared for these roles? Can I aid in the preparation?

Preventive intervention programs are also needed in school systems when an unusual event is anticipated which will cause role expectations to change rapidly; the onset of a desegregation program is an obvious example. A research study conducted with youngsters involved in such a program revealed that the children did not know how to cope with situations in which they wished to invite the child of another race to their homes but were certain that their parents would not approve. They did not know how to interpret their friendship with a child of another race to peers who considered them "traitors to the gang." The teachers were equally unprepared for the new demands upon them. They were not prepared to handle behavior problems they had never encountered before or to manage expressions of racial prejudice by the students. The administration had hoped that by ignoring problematic situations, difficulties would be avoided. This strategy was not successful, as it seldom is.

Other examples of situations that can be predicted to cause disruptions as a result of changing role expectations are the onset of decentralization programs, student demands for increased power, and the introduction of modular scheduling which gives the students blocks of times when they are relatively unsupervised.

In planning programs which facilitate the transition to new roles or adaptation to changing demands in old roles, the school social worker's task should be to analyze the new demands that will be made, assess the skills and knowledge that will be required, and then develop a training program that will enable the target population to fill those demands. It is not assumed that the social worker will personally conduct all of these programs. Wherever possible, other individuals should be involved: paraprofessionals, students, teachers, members of the local community, graduates of former training programs. Nor should it be assumed that the entire burden of change should fall upon the novice or the individual who is experiencing changing role demands. It is also important that the school system make adjustments to ease the fit of person and role. Thus, it is essential that the school social worker make recommendations to administrators about systemic changes that are needed. A few examples have already been alluded to. Time and room must be allowed for a buddy system to function. Support for an in-service training program for teachers is needed. High school students must be given time and transportation to visit places of employment. In Piagetian terms, both assimilation and accommodation are needed if preventive intervention programs are to function effectively. The individual must change to be assimilated into the system, and the system must be modified to accommodate the novice.

School social work is not limited to treating the child who presents problems in the school, or to treating groups of children who present problems in school, or even to treating problems per

Preventive Intervention through the School

se. The role must also include problem prevention, whether focusing on the four-year-old child who is unprepared for kindergarten or on the teacher who is unprepared to handle racial conflict in her class. Before engaging in preventive intervention programs, however, the school social worker will have to stop thinking of himself solely as a therapist diagnosing and treating ailing patients. The problems that schools face today are far too complex and abundant to permit that restricted a view. A broader perspective of school social work is needed, and no one is putting blinders on school social workers except school social workers themselves.

Addiction

CHARLES LONG

IF I WERE ASKED what are some of the things that are instrumental in people becoming addicts, my answer would read something like this: I would think that his personality has a great deal to do with a person's becoming an addict. Also, the environment from which one comes plays an important part in helping to push one into the entanglements of drugs. Maybe even his parental influences and religious doctrines can also be motivating factors. Definitely, there is an emotional factor that leads to the use of drugs. I mention these things because I think they are the most important of all reasons for a person to get involved with narcotics.

Of course, there are those who acquire the habit through medical treatment, but the number is few. Drugs are given very carefully nowadays by doctors who know the consequence of addiction. There are those who stumble into drug addiction by using barbiturates to help them sleep, or other drugs to bring relief from the tensions of a hard day's work, or to ease nervous conditions of different kinds.

I became an addict at the age of sixteen. Not everyone becomes an addict at such an early age. I was not a rare case, however, for there are many such as myself who became addicts in their teens. There were no pushers hanging around my school, as we are led to believe by those who just look at addiction from the legal standpoint. Pushers did not hang around trying to get kids on the stuff, enticing them for the benefits of a dollar. That come-on-get-high thing is plastered in newspapers, on television and radio, and all the vicious lies are told to the misguided jurors when an addict is on trial. These ideas are disseminated by the police,

Addiction

district attorneys, commercial magazines, and other narrow groups, supposedly for the benefit of the public.

A kid has to be looking for something when he gets involved with drugs. This can come by way of a great many things, broken homes, distorted values, emotional maladjustments, and so forth. If whiskey offered the stimulation that the youth feels will aid him in the escape from the confusion and very unpredictable confrontations of youth, then he turns to whatever there is to bring satisfaction. I hope I made myself clear when I mentioned certain ideas that have not been classically established as the main causes of addiction. Maybe I should have tried to paint an emotional picture of myself in reference to the addiction problem. Cases and reasons for using narcotics differ, the personality make-up is different in each individual.

I think that children have always had a problem in growing up. Youth will always be plagued with some kind of problem. A child can come up in the worse kind of an environment and yet never use drugs. By the same token, a child from the very best environment can use drugs and fall into the same situation as the child in the worst environment.

You may wonder what all of this has to do with addiction. I think what I have mentioned may serve as an introduction into the world of drugs and the reason for their use and continuance in this world of make-believe. You see, drugs are addictive in two ways, mental and physical, with the mental being the things that are binding in mind and feelings toward the continued use of drugs. Now, to me, the physical addiction starts out in the form of kicks. After two or three weeks of shooting these drugs into your veins, your body builds up a tolerance, and when you cannot get the drugs after you have the habit, you get very sick.

The sickness is one of the most horrible of all sicknesses. You have the "monkey on your back," you yawn and get a terrible sickness in the pit of your stomach. Your eyes and nose start to run; later, your bowels break. You get this twitching feeling all over your body. Every bone in the body starts to ache, and you have cold sweats. If you do not get the drugs that your body craves, you get even sicker. This sickness usually lasts about seven days. During the sickness nothing will stay on your stomach, there is no sleep, and you constantly vomit. At first you vomit all the food and liquids you had in the stomach before getting sick. The vomiting becomes dry after the second day. There is an unpleasant body odor caused by the film that the cold sweats have left on your body.

After seven days of this sort of hell, the addict can start eating again. In just a few days, he can consume a large amount of food, particularly sweets, for he has sweated out most if not all of the sugars and salts of the body. Although he is still unable to get a peaceful night's sleep, he slowly comes back to normal in his other habits. The mental craving is still there, although there is no physical need for the drug. At night, most addicts dream about drugs; during the day they think about them constantly. Drugs have become to them like food is to a hungry person, or like water to someone who has gone for days without it.

Let us now talk about a way in which addiction can be curbed. Why not start making it a part of our teaching programs in schools for new teachers, who will teach the kids of tomorrow? Why not have classes for the P.T.A. members? This will enlighten them so that they may help fight the sickness that may entrap their kids and other loved ones. Have a doctor speak before the kids, their parents, to churches, and to other groups. Let us use public relations to bring forth the facts discovered by men who are studying the problem and who have knowledge of drug addiction. Then concentrate on the newspaper editorials so that they will shed light on addiction. Set up more funds and research laboratories to find a solution that will be beneficial to the addict as well as to society. Stop allowing the police, the courts, and the legal wheels from giving out information that a qualified person should give or try to correct. Let the policeman be just what he is, the lawyer a lawyer, so as not to slow down progress in treating the addicts and ridding society of this disease. Let the schools, churches, and other organizations educate on this as they do on venereal diseases, as they do on the many other sicknesses for which they teach preventive measures.

I would like to make a plea for the addict.

Addiction

Show us the right way. We want and need to change. If you only knew how badly we want to belong! Lend us your hand, give us hope for a better tomorrow. We do not want appeasement; we want to belong to the brighter things of real value. The door has been closed too long to us who have strayed.

Invite us into your hearts. Let us take the same pleasure that you would offer a child who has been lost to the devil (that white powder). Open the doors of your home as you have the prison gates. Make the burden a little easier to carry by trying to understand our sickness. We do not say that we are the only people who are sick, but we are the only ones who are punished for our sickness. Instead of being sent to a hospital where we can be treated for this sickness, we are sent to prison in this modern country for long and unreasonable sentences. Sure, crimes are committed because of drugs, or rather to attain them. Crimes are also committed for countless other reasons, crimes much more serious than those committed to maintain a habit. This is not to justify the position of the addict; by the same token, this is not to focus attention on the nonaddict. We are asking for help because we do not like our way of life, and we agree that it costs the country a great deal of money in all aspects of the principles on which the country is based. Spend some money to stop this malignant disease, spend some money to educate the public in an understanding manner, not in the hard and vicious way that has been done in the past. Let there be a board of physicians, specialists, social workers, and other professionals. Research in the next five or ten years might possibly come up with something, if there is such a program. Include the law, of course, but not in the sense of penalty where there is no real need. Let them work with the doctors and those who have been trained to look into the sickness of these seemingly helpless people. Politics should have no part in this organization unless it is for the good of all concerned and not just to win an election.

Something has got to be done, someone has got to hear the call in the night, the plea of the addict. He cannot find success without the knowledge that you will accept him after changes have been made. He is nothing unless you make him know that there is hope for him. It is so important to know that understanding and love are part of the prize that awaits him from the pits of hell. Salvation can only be found by the addict in you; until he can feel that you will forgive him, there is no peace for him. Deep within, he loves and admires you for your strength and ability to face the realities of everyday living. So we the addicts beg you: give us your hand, lend your hearts and minds to the horror that the addict has to live with.

Index

"Activism," 41
Activist, administrative, 50-52
"Addiction," 198-202
"Administrative activism," 50
Advocacy, 65-73
Aged, individualized treatment of the mentally impaired, 89-102; mental impairment of the, 92-93
"Alleviating Tensions in an Ethnic Neighborhood," 54-64
Alta House (Cleveland), 54, 60-63
Argyris, Chris, cited, 26
Aronin, Geraldine, cited, 103

Balzer, Gary, cited, 103
"Bases of Social Treatment, The," 149-77
"Beyond Advocacy: a New Model for Community Organization," 65-73
Billingsley, Andrew, cited, 121, 123
Bion, W. R., cited, 28
Black culture, adaptive aspects of, 121-24
Bowles, Dorcas L., quoted, 125
Brager, George A., quoted, 51, 67
Brody, Elaine, paper by, 89-102; cited, 89-90, 101; quoted, 100
Bronfenbrenner, Urie, cited, 184

Casework practice, 149-50; race in, 114-26
Chaiklin, Harris, paper by, 103-13; cited, 104
Chestang, Leon W., paper by, 114-26
Children, day care for, 127-48
Citizen participation, 17-18, 19-20
Cleaver, Eldridge, quoted, 41; cited, 57
Cleveland, Alta House, 54, 60-63; Little Italy, 57-59; tensions in an ethnic neighborhood, 54-64

"Client, Staff, and the Social Agency," 21-40
Client self-determination, 66, 67
Client system: composition of, 168-69; nature of, 166-68; structure of, 170
Client-worker system: composition of, 164-68; processes of, 174
Cloward, Richard A., quoted, 19
Cobbs, Price M., quoted, 117
Cole, Charlotte, cited, 89
Coles, Robert, cited, 117
Collins, Alice H., cited, 132
Columbia Spectator, 84
Community organization, 3, 65-73
Community Organization and Services to Improve Family Living Project, 103, 108-12
Compensatory justice, 10
Confidentiality, in social research, 77-79
"Conservative Strategy for Social Planning in the Seventies, A," 3-20
Corsellis, J. A. N., quoted, 92

Day Care and Child Development Council of America, 130
Day care: neighborhood family day care, 129-32, 133-36; realistic planning for consumer of, 127-48
Denver Plan, 178
Detroit, preventive intervention program, 192-93
Dissensus politics, 12
Drug addiction, 198-202

Early Education Program (Ypsilanti, Mich.), 191-92
Education for social work: group field work and tutorial experience, 178-82
Emlen, Arthur C., paper by, 127-42
Epstein, Irwin, cited, 50

"Ethical and Political Issues in Social Research," 74-88
Ethnic groups, 55-57
Ethnic neighborhoods, alleviating tensions in, 54-64
Etzioni, Amitai, cited, 11; quoted, 15

Field Study of the Neighborhood Family Day Care System (Portland, Oreg.), 132, 133, 138, 141
Follett, Mary Parker, cited, 53
Ford Foundation, grey areas programs of, 3
French, John R. P., Jr., cited, 171
"From Social Work to Social Administration," 41-53
Fryman, Evelyn, cited, 96

Galinsky, Maeda, cited, 175
Garfield, Goodwin, quoted, 38
Garvin, Charles, paper by, 149-77
Gilmer, Barbara, cited, 184
Glasser, Paul, paper by, 149-77
Grass, Günter, cited, 105; quoted, 106-7
Greeley, Andrew M., quoted, 55
Grier, William H., quoted, 117
Grosser, Charles F., cited, 66, 68
"Group Field Work and Tutorial Experience," 178-82
Group work, as habilitation method, 152-53

Hanlan, Archie, paper by, 41-53
Harrington, Michael, cited, 50
Heilbroner, Robert L., quoted, 9
Hernton, Calvin C., cited, 57
Hinds County (Miss.) welfare rights movement, 71-72
HJA, see Home for the Jewish Aged
Hoffman, Lyn, cited, 31
Home for the Jewish Aged (HJA) (Philadelphia), individualized treatment of the mentally impaired in, 89-102
Hopkins, Harry, quoted, 107
Hughes, Langston, quoted, 113
Hunt, William, cited, 52

"Individualized Treatment of the Mentally Impaired Aged," 89-102
Institutional change, and liberal planners, 6-7
Integration, in schools, 6
Intervention: preventive, 182-97; sequence in practice, 157-64
Isaacs, Harold R., quoted, 115
"Issue of Race in Casework Practice, The," 114-26

Jacobson, L., cited, 192

Kadushin, Charles, cited, 83
Kahn, Alfred J., cited, 11; quoted, 5, 8, 186
Kahn, Robert L., cited, 45, 46
Kahn, Robert S., cited, 94
Kahn-Goldfarb-Pollack Mental Status Questionnaire, 95
Karnes, M., cited, 184
Katz, Martin M., cited, 85
Khinduka, S. K., cited, 42; quoted, 45, 47
Kirby, Betty A., paper by, 178-82
Kleban, Morton H., cited, 89, 101
Krickus, Richard J., cited, 57
Kurzman, Paul A., paper by, 65-73; cited, 69

Laing, R. D., quoted, 116
Lawton, M. Powell, cited, 89, 94; quoted, 93-94
Lewin, Kurt, cited, 21
Liebowitz, Bernard, cited, 89-90; quoted, 100
Lindsay, John V., quoted, 107-8
Little Italy (Cleveland), 57-59
Long, Charles, paper by, 198-202
Long, Lorence, cited, 31
Low-income families, preventive intervention with, 183-97

Malinowski, Bronislaw Kasper, cited, 178-79
Mayer, Anna B., cited, 135
Medicare, 105
Mental health: individualized treatment of mentally impaired aged, 89-102; mental impairment of the aged, 92-93
Michael Schwerner Memorial Fund, 68, 72
Mikulski, Barbara, cited, 103
Milgram, Stanley, cited 75-76
Mobilization for Youth, 3
Monroe, Mich., preventive intervention program, 192

Index

Moynihan, Daniel P., cited, 50; quoted, 10, 15

National Association of Social Workers (NASW), 46, 52; survey on job functions, 43
National development, 47
National Federation of Settlements and Neighborhood Centers, 54-55
National Welfare Rights Organization, 72
"*Negeya* bond," 69, 70-71
Negroes: black culture, 121-24; deprived status of, 115-18
Neighborhood service centers, 3
"New citizenship," 17, 18
"New politics," 16-17

Oakland, Calif., family day care in, 134
Olson, Glenn W., paper by, 54-64
Operation Alphabet (Philadelphia), 137, 142-43

Perry, Joseph B., cited, 131
Pfaff, William, quoted, 4, 7
Philadelphia: Home for the Jewish Aged, 89-102; Office of Family Service, 143; Operation Alphabet, 137, 142-43; Philadelphia County Board of Assistance, 132, 143; Philadelphia Geriatric Center, 89-90
Pittman, Audrey, paper by, 142-48
Piven, Frances Fox, quoted, 19
Planning, see Social planning
Plymouth, Mich., program with lower-class fathers, 193-94
Portland (Oreg.) Day Care Neighbor Service, 139; Field Study, 132-33, 141-42
Poverty amid Plenty; the American Paradox, quoted, 104
President's Commission on Income Maintenance Programs, 104, 105
"Preventive Intervention with Low-Income Families through the School," 183-97
Public welfare, social service team for, 103-13

Race, in casework practice, 114-26
Radin, Norma, paper by, 183-97; cited, 183, 184, 191

Raven, Bertram H., cited, 171
"Realistic Planning for the Day Care Consumer," 127-48
Research: confidentiality in, 77-79; definition of social problems, 81-82; demonstrations, 79-81; ethical and political issues, 74-88; informed consent, 84; invasion of privacy, 76-77; resistance of subjects, 83-84; restraint in, 86-88; use of results, 82
Resources, mobilization of, for social change, 13-15
Rosenthal, R., cited, 192
Ross, David F., quoted, 8
Roszak, Theodore, cited, 14
Rothman, Jack, cited, 44, 50
Ruderman, Florence A., cited, 134, 135, 138, 139; quoted, 136

Sample, William C., cited, 103
Sarri, Rosemary C., cited, 45-46, 157, 175
Sawyer, Jack, cited, 79
Schechter, Howard, cited, 78
Schools: integration in, 6; low-income children and the, 183; preventive intervention through, 183-97
School social work, 183-97
Schorr, Alvin L., quoted, 100
Schwartz, Edward E., quoted, 103
Schwartz, William, cited, 28, 29; quoted, 25, 30, 33
Sensitivity training, 26
Shick, Allen, cited, 47, 48
Shulman, Lawrence, paper by, 21-40; cited, 33
Silverman, Herbert A., paper by, 89-102; cited, 101
Social action, 3
Social administration, 47-49; and social work, 41-53
Social agency: administration, 23-25; client and staff, 21-40; communication problems, 25-26; executive, 29-30, 37-38; myth and reality in, 23-29; professionalism in, 29-40; as a social system, 22-23; supervisory, 29, 33-37; worker, 24-25, 26-29, 30-33, 38-39
Social change, 18; in a cybernetic society, 12-13; mobilization of resources for, 13-15
Social planning, 3-20; and authority, 9; and conservatives, 5; and liberal view,

Social planning *(Continued)*
  5, 6, 10; and psychological theories, 5-6; value judgments in, 5
"Social Service Team for Public Welfare, A," 103-13
Social welfare: administration, 45-47; resources, 52-53
Social work, 4, 5, 18; administration in, 43-45; and social administration, 41-53
Social work practice: bases of social treatment in, 149-77; client system, 168-73; client-worker system, 164-68, 174-77; and goal determination, 158-59; intervention sequence, 157-64, with mentally impaired aged, 99-102; and race, 114-26; in schools, 183-97; in social agencies, 21-40; worker as organizer-advocate in, 68-69; worker as organizer-educator in, 69-71; worker as organizer-technical assistant in, 71-73
Solomon, Jeffrey R., paper by, 65-73
Stein, Bette, cited, 103
Stokes, Carl B., 58, 63

T—groups, 26
Tutorial experience, and group field work, 178-82

University of Denver, 178
University of Michigan School of Social Work, 154

Value judgments, in social planning, 5
Vinter, Robert D., cited, 161

Waldman, Arthur, 89; cited, 96
Weiss, Carol H., paper by, 74-88
Weissman, Harold H., paper by, 3-20; cited, 10
Westin, Alan F., quoted, 79
Wilde, Oscar, cited, 9
Willner, Milton, cited, 132, 139
Wittes, Glorianne, cited, 191

Ypsilanti, Mich., Early Education Program, 191-92; intervention program, 193

Zald, Mayer N., cited, 66

Other Papers from the 97th Annual Forum

Papers presented at the 97th Annual Forum may also be found in *The Social Welfare Forum, 1970,* published by Columbia University Press:

Social Welfare Priorities for the 1970s,   *Wilbur J. Cohen*
The Family Assistance Plan—the Nixon Proposal   *John D. Twiname*
Income-Security Policies—the Heineman Commission Proposal   *Barbara Jordan*
A Critique of the Family Assistance Plan   *George McGovern*
Income Maintenance and the Social Security Ideology   *Alvin L. Schorr*
Welfare Reform and Income Security Policies   *Eveline M. Burns*
Moral and Ethical Issues in Income Maintenance
    I. A Protestant Viewpoint   *Victor Obenhaus*
    II. A Catholic Viewpoint   *Rev. Robert Kennedy*
Decision-Makers in Social Policy   *Alan K. Campbell*
Institutionalized Racism in Social Welfare Agencies   *Dan W. Dodson*
Social Change or Service Delivery?   *Robert R. Mayer*
Neighborhoods and Social Policy: Continuities and Discontinuities with the Past
    Daniel M. Fox

CONFRONTATION, 1970
Social Welfare Priorities—a Minority View   *T. George Silcott*
Where Are Solutions?   *Virginia R. Doscher*
Chicago Scene I: Conference Report   *Werner H. Boehm*
Chicago Scene II: Report from a Participant   *Howard E. Prunty*
National Conference on Social Welfare: a Report to the Membership
    New York to Chicago: Conference Report
    New York to Chicago: an Observer's Comment   *Florence Horchow*